ELVIS PRESLEY

★ ★ ★ ★ ★ ★ ★ ★ ★ ★ ★ ★ ★ ★ ★ ★ ★ ★

POP CULTURE LEGENDS

ELVIS PRESLEY

★ ★ ★ ★ ★ ★ ★ ★ ★ ★ ★ ★ ★ ★ ★ ★

TONY GENTRY

CHELSEA HOUSE PUBLISHERS

New York ★ Philadelphia

CHELSEA HOUSE PUBLISHERS

EDITORIAL DIRECTOR   Richard Rennert
EXECUTIVE MANAGING EDITOR   Karyn Gullen Browne
COPY CHIEF   Robin James
PICTURE EDITOR   Adrian G. Allen
ART DIRECTOR   Robert Mitchell
MANUFACTURING DIRECTOR   Gerald Levine

Pop Culture Legends
SENIOR EDITOR   Kathy Kuhtz Campbell
SERIES DESIGN   Basia Niemczyc

Staff for **ELVIS PRESLEY**
ASSOCIATE EDITOR   Martin Schwabacher
EDITORIAL ASSISTANT   Kelsey Goss
PICTURE RESEARCHER   Wendy P. Wills
COVER ILLUSTRATION   Daniel Mark Duffy

5   7   9   8   6

Library of Congress Cataloging-in-Publication Data

Gentry, Tony.
Elvis Presley/Tony Gentry
p. cm.—(Pop culture legends)
Includes bibliographical references and index.
ISBN 0-7910-2329-X.
        0-7910-2354-0 (pbk.)
1. Presley, Elvis, 1935–1977—Juvenile literature. 2. Rock sing-
ers—United States—Biography—Juvenile literature. [1. Presley,
Elvis, 1935–1977. 2. Singers. 3. Rock music.] I. Title.
ML3930.P73G43 1994   93-28486
782.42166'092—dc20   CIP
[B]   AC MN

FRONTISPIECE:
A smiling Elvis Presley relaxes on his sofa.

Contents ★ ★ ★ ★ ★ ★ ★ ★ ★ ★ ★ ★ ★ ★ ★ ★ ★ ★

A Reflection of Ourselves

Leeza Gibbons

I ENJOY A RARE PERSPECTIVE on the entertainment industry. From my window on popular culture, I can see all that sizzles and excites. I have interviewed legends who have left us, such as Bette Davis and Sammy Davis, Jr., and have brushed shoulders with the names who have caused a commotion with their sheer outrageousness, like Boy George and Madonna. Whether it's by nature or by design, pop icons generate interest, and I think they are a mirror of who we are at any given time.

Who are *your* heroes and heroines, the people you most admire? Outside of your own family and friends, to whom do you look for inspiration and guidance, as examples of the type of person you would like to be as an adult? How do we decide who will be the most popular and influential members of our society?

You may be surprised by your answers. According to recent polls, you will probably respond much differently than your parents or grandparents did to the same questions at the same age. Increasingly, world leaders such as Winston Churchill, John F. Kennedy, Franklin D. Roosevelt, and evangelist Billy Graham have been replaced by entertainers, athletes, and popular artists as the individuals whom young people most respect and admire. In surveys taken during each of the past 15 years, for example, General Norman Schwarzkopf was the only world leader chosen as the number-one hero among high school students. Other names on the elite list joined by General Schwarzkopf included Paula Abdul, Michael Jackson, Michael Jordan, Eddie Murphy, Burt Reynolds, and Sylvester Stallone.

More than 30 years have passed since Canadian sociologist Marshall McLuhan first taught us the huge impact that the electronic media has had on how we think, learn, and understand—as well as how we choose our heroes. In the 1960s, Pop artist Andy Warhol predicted that there would soon come a time when every American would be famous for 15 minutes. But if it is easier today to achieve Warhol's 15 minutes of fame, it is also much harder to hold on to it. Reputations are often ruined as quickly as they are made.

And yet, there remain those artists and performers who continue to inspire and instruct us in spite of changes in world events, media technology, or popular tastes. Even in a society as fickle and fast moving as our own, there are still those performers whose work and reputation endure, pop culture legends who inspire an almost religious devotion from their fans.

Why do the works and personalities of some artists continue to fascinate us while others are so quickly forgotten? What, if any, qualities do they share that enable them to have such power over our lives? There are no easy answers to these questions. The artists and entertainers profiled in this series often have little more in common than the enormous influence that each of them has had on our lives.

Some offer us an escape. Artists such as actress Marilyn Monroe, comedian Groucho Marx, and writer Stephen King have used glamour, humor, or fantasy to help us escape from our everyday lives. Others present us with images that are all too recognizable. The uncompromising realism of actor and director Charlie Chaplin and folk singer Bob Dylan challenges us to confront and change the things in our world that most disturb us.

Some offer us friendly, reassuring experiences. The work of animator Walt Disney and late-night talk show host Johnny Carson, for example, provides us with a sense of security and continuity in a changing world. Others shake us up. The best work of composer John Lennon and actor James Dean will always inspire their fans to question and reevaluate the world in which they live.

It is also hard to predict the kind of life that a pop culture legend will lead, or how he or she will react to fame. Popular singers Michael Jackson

and Prince carefully guard their personal lives from public view. Other performers, such as popular singer Madonna, enjoy putting their private lives before the public eye.

What these artists and entertainers do share, however, is the rare ability to capture and hold the public's imagination in a world dominated by mass media and disposable celebrity. In spite of their differences, each of them has somehow managed to achieve legendary status in a popular culture that values novelty and change.

The books in this series examine the lives and careers of these and other pop culture legends, and the society that places such great value on their work. Each book considers the extraordinary talent, the stubborn commitment, and the great personal sacrifice required to create work of enduring quality and influence in today's world.

As you read these books, ask yourself the following questions: How are the careers of these individuals shaped by their society? What role do they play in shaping the world? And what is it that so captivates us about their lives, their work, or the images they present?

Hopefully, by studying the lives and achievements of these pop culture legends, we will learn more about ourselves.

Rip It Up

I T TOOK ELVIS PRESLEY just 1 minute and 56 seconds to change the world. When the young singer from Memphis, Tennessee, appeared on national television on June 5, 1956, to perform a rhythm-and-blues tune called "Hound Dog" that he had stripped down and speeded up like a hot rod jalopy, the rock 'n' roll era was born.

Looking back now, when the revolution that Presley spawned permeates popular culture, it may be hard to understand how radical the changes he wrought actually were. But in the spring of 1956, the world was a very different place.

The United States of Presley's youth had emerged from World War II as the most powerful nation in the world, and the government had used its power on the home front to provide subsidies for returning soldiers so they could go to college, buy houses, and start careers and families. The suburbs that span the nation today were built from scratch in those years. With thousands of war veterans starting families all at once, the national population exploded, creating what was soon dubbed the Baby Boom.

Elvis Presley demonstrates his unique ability to bewitch an audience. The surging fans at this performance on July 5, 1956, had to be restrained by police and fire fighters.

At the same time, the United States and the Soviet Union had begun to build awesome hydrogen bombs, threatening the world with instant annihilation. At the sound of air-raid sirens, students across the country learned to duck beneath their desks in a feeble effort to protect themselves from nuclear bombs. War veterans who had fought to make the world a safer place now found themselves building bomb shelters in their basements, attempting to make safe havens for their families at home.

Thanks to the recent invention of stereo and television, anyone could replicate concert sound in their own home or get news, religion, entertainment, or exercise tips on-screen at the turn of a knob. The new technology quickly created a nation of homebodies. In 1950 there were only 1.5 million TV sets in the United States. By the time Elvis Presley appeared on television six years later, more than 50 million families had them.

The early TV programs were always safe and predictable. The biggest name in television, Ed Sullivan, provided a mix of jugglers, comics, animal acts, puppets, and singers on his weekly variety show, "Toast of the Town." Comedians Milton Berle and Steve Allen did the same on their programs. Most variety shows had 30-piece big bands, whose muted horns provided sedate orchestral sound tracks for the silly skits on-screen. Announcers wore tuxedos; dancers dressed like show girls. Even the "live" shows seemed canned.

Parents wanted mildly interesting family entertainment on their new black-and-white consoles, nothing that would overstimulate the kids or ruffle the feathers of their grandparents. For the most part, that is what the few available TV channels provided. Bored and restless teenagers, on the other hand, idolized rebellious movie stars, such as Marlon Brando and James Dean, who seemed to understand their frustration at being trapped in such a straitlaced environment. Author Jack Kerouac celebrated a complete rejection of America's obsession with stable jobs, families, and communities in favor of a life of reckless wandering. His daring novel *On the Road* (1957) became a sort of Bible for nonconformist teenagers who wanted more out of life than a homemaking career like their mother's or a job like their father's. But none of them imagined that a hero could appear on the televisions in their own living rooms.

In January 1956, "The Stage Show," hosted by aging big band leaders Tommy and Jimmy Dorsey, was about to be booted off the air. In desperation, the brothers hired a novelty act from Memphis, Tennessee, a young man whose strangely affecting blues record "Heartbreak

Tommy and Jimmy Dorsey typified the performers on television in the 1950s. The genial big-band musicians offered Elvis his first big break on television with a guest spot on their weekly variety show, "The Stage Show," in January 1956.

Hotel" had just been released. The Dorseys did not expect much from a singer they considered a hillbilly; they hired him to fill up time between skits. This is how Elvis Presley's music was unleashed into the nation's living rooms, without any warning.

The show opened with its usual slick orchestral theme music. The Dorsey brothers, looking old and paunchy in their cummerbunds, bowed to the tiny studio audience before introducing the new act. The camera then swept over their orchestra. Stolid musicians sat like neat rows of penguins behind music-stand boxes, blowing a saccharine melody.

Suddenly a rough-looking guy with a big guitar strode onstage and headed right past the band without even a nod of thanks. No tuxedo for him; he was wearing a boxy sportscoat, a black shirt, and a widely knotted white tie. Glistening hair sprouted up wildly at his forehead. The lights dimmed on the big band, so they seemed to completely disappear, and now the only things on-screen were the young man with the guitar, pausing before a huge microphone stand, and his three-piece band featuring electric guitar, upright bass, and meager drum set.

Presley shrugged to start the song. Somehow, his little band seemed louder than all of Dorsey's hornmen. They sounded rough-hewn, plodding, hard to figure. It could be hillbilly music, it could be blues, but it was too fast for either. The singer's acoustic rhythm guitar was the biggest sound of all, nervous and driven. Presley's face appeared flat, unformed, and brutal, but there was a soulful pain in his heavily lidded eyes and a leering sensuality in his smile. Just as astonishing as his music, however, was the way he moved.

As Presley sang, the guitar went one way, his neck snapped back the other, and his lips seemed torn between the two directions. The lyrics to the song, "Blue Suede Shoes," written by another Memphis singer, Carl

Perkins, were a teenager's yelping cry for respect. After defiantly shouting his demand that no one step on his shoes, the singer dropped back like a quarterback to be surrounded by his bandmates. While the electric guitarist picked a biting, whiny solo, Presley's legs went into a strange, gangly spasm that revealed white socks to match his gleaming smile.

Then he lurched back to the microphone again. He looked completely casual, as if he was chewing gum and singing at the same time. The words were coming so hard, complete with hiccups, stutters, crossed eyes, and quick swoops up the musical scale, that the singer seemed to be leaning out the window of a speeding truck and wailing into the wind. As the song came to a close, he fell back with his eyes closed, his bandmates threw their arms up awkwardly, and Presley bowed so quickly it was almost a blur.

The studio audience just sat there, stunned. Someone squealed for an instant. Eventually people clapped, hesitantly. Presley left the stage looking puzzled.

The Dorseys seemed amused at least, hiring Presley for five more performances. With each show more people tuned in, as word spread about this energetic young wild man. But it was not until June 5, when Presley appeared on the popular "Milton Berle Show," that the nation really sat up and took notice. By that time Presley's song "Heartbreak Hotel" had topped the pop, country, and rhythm-and-blues radio playlists. More people watched Presley on Berle's program than on all of the Dorsey appearances combined. He did not disappoint them.

Presley strode onstage this time looking even more casual, without a guitar or a necktie. The band stood stiffly behind him in dark suits with small bow ties. The singer grabbed the heavy microphone stand between thumb and forefinger as if it weighed nothing, tipping

The reckless physical abandon and provocative sexuality of Elvis's dancing shocked and thrilled audiences in the 1950s.

it off its base. Suddenly his arms pumped the air, one knee kicked in at the other, and the expectant quiet of the studio was shattered by the first line of his newest song, shouted so quickly it sounded like one word: "You ain't nothin' but a hound dog!"

Before the audience could catch its breath, the guitarist unleashed a loud, metallic solo. Presley shuffled sideways toward him as if drawn to the music against his will, seemingly surprised at his own dance. The guitarist bore down heavily on the strings, with Presley nodding enraptured beside him. Suddenly Presley leaped back to the microphone and began to speed up the verse. He grinned at his own legs as they flew into seemingly uncontrolled spasms. He stepped on his pants cuffs and laughed. Now the camera turned to the audience, a crowd of young people in prim Sunday clothes. Some faces showed bewilderment, some disgust, others outright laughter or stunned surprise.

With no warning, Presley leaped to the right side of the screen, almost falling on his knees. He caught himself on toe-point, dragging the teetering microphone stand. It was a dazzling, totally spontaneous move, like nothing anyone had seen on television before. The band stopped. The song—which had been careening breathlessly along for a whole minute—was suddenly over.

Presley reeled backward, practically offscreen, using the microphone stand for balance. He was not through yet. Like a comic-book super-hero hit by a stun ray, he pointed back to the right and bent his knees on tip-toe, frozen. The band looked surprised. And here came those strange, put-down lyrics again, tortuously slow this time as he pumped his hips with each word: "You—ain't—a—nothin'—but—a—hoouunndd—dog—a!" Now his shoulders shrugged like he was being shoved hard from behind by the drumbeat. His upper body aped the hunchbacks and zombies of the current drive-in movies while his legs whipped like rubber. He was laughing at his own reckless mischief and singing up a storm. Before the last echo of the guitar

When Elvis appeared on "The Steve Allen Show" on July 1, 1956, the host made Elvis sing his fiery hit song "Hound Dog" to a basset hound.

faded, the buck-toothed visage of host Milton Berle burst on-screen, whistling with fingers in his teeth and shouting, "Elvis Presley! I love him! I love him!" The singer gazed ecstatically up at the stage lights. In 1 minute and 56 seconds he had kicked the stale music of television big bands in the teeth, shown the nation's youth that they had life below the waist, terrified their parents, pulled together musical traditions as different as blues and country, and suggested previously undreamed of possibilities for fun and excitement to anyone with ears to hear. Maybe Presley did not know all of this at the time as he panted breathlessly before the commercial break. But he seemed plainly amazed at his own daring.

The nation's cultural guardians struck back the next day. Critic John Crosby of the *New York Herald Tribune* called Presley "unspeakably untalented and vulgar." A radio wit dubbed the singer "Elvis the Pelvis" because of his suggestive stage moves. Church congregations mailed petitions to Milton Berle demanding an apology for presenting such an ungodly example to the nation's youth. Popular TV host Ed Sullivan declared that Presley would never appear on *his* show.

The millions of teenagers who had been watching Presley's TV performances did not need critics to explain what they had seen. His band's driving beat, its loud chaotic guitar solos, and Presley's manic stage moves, sly humor, and hiccuped singing made sense to them as nothing else ever had. This kind of energy seemed too big to be packaged on a TV show. Their parents may have been fuming with disgust, but Presley's music made young people want to dance and shout.

With that, the much discussed "Generation Gap" was born. As biographer Dave Marsh writes, "Not even the most silver-tongued teenager could have explained the alchemy of Elvis to an unconvinced adult. You either saw it or you didn't. It split the country." Presley's performances came as a liberating rallying cry, proclaiming the sheer joy of cutting loose from adult constraints.

When Presley and his bandmates took the train from Memphis to New York to perform on comedian Steve Allen's "Tonight Show" in July, teenage girls lined up at every station along the way, screaming, waving placards, and clawing at the windows of the passing train. The bravest of these girls put on their best poodle skirts and saddle oxfords, tied their hair up in pony tails, and dared to buy tickets to actually ride the train from one stop to the next in hopes of seeing their new idol. From his private berth, Presley peeked past the curtains at the commotion he was causing. His bandmates chuckled in amazement.

Comedian Steve Allen had decided that the best way to deal with the commotion was to make fun of it. He wanted to nip Presley's blossoming rock 'n' roll music in the bud. So he talked the young singer into putting on a tuxedo. Then he had Presley stand onstage amid glitzy candelabras while his bandmates were shoved far to the back of the stage. Finally, he brought out a game old basset hound wearing a top hat and sitting on a bar stool. Presley had to sing his new hit, "Hound Dog," to the poor beast.

The song that had seemed so wild and volatile one month before on "The Milton Berle Show" now came across as a lame novelty tune. Presley tried his best to be a good sport about the whole thing, peering lovingly into the dog's droopy eyes and giving the dog a boyish hug at the end, but it was plain that he was angry and embarrassed by the whole stunt.

A crowd in Memphis, Tennessee, goes wild at the premiere of Elvis's second movie, *Loving You,* on July 9, 1957. The hysteria with which Presley's audiences responded to his performances alarmed many adults in the conservative 1950s.

For his second song, Allen took the dog away. Presley tugged at his bow tie and sang a yearning romantic ballad, "I Want You, I Need You, I Love You." This performance surprised critics who had thought he could only shake his hips and shout. But Allen's strategy made it clear that the old guard of swing musicians and nightclub performers who ruled television were not going to roll over and play dead for Presley's new music. They would do what it took to make his scintillating performances seem just as staid and old-fashioned as their own.

Finally, in September, Ed Sullivan—the most important TV host of all—relented from his pledge that Presley would never appear on his show. By that time Presley had three top-10 hits on radio playlists and could no longer be ignored. Sullivan paid the singer $50,000 for three appearances, an unprecedented sum at the time. But Sullivan's investment paid off when 82 percent of the American families that owned televisions—54 million people—tuned in to watch.

On his September 9 appearance, Presley seemed determined to overcome the humiliation suffered at the hands of Steve Allen. Wearing a knobby-textured checked jacket without a tie and playing an ornately decorated cowboy acoustic guitar, he introduced a brand new rock 'n' roll song, "Ready Teddy." The band now included a pianist and a quartet of male backup singers, the Jordanaires. In crew cuts and bow ties, the middle-aged Jordanaires did their best to keep up with the music, but when Presley pounded into the high-velocity chorus, "I'm ready ready Teddy to rock 'n' roll!" they stopped dead with their jaws agape, unable to follow the beat.

Presley laughed and charged on. By this time—after six TV appearances in as many months—he had figured out exactly how to use the television screen. He froze midsong, waited for the girls in the audience to scream, grinned, and wailed the next line. When he crossed his eyes at a high note, the teenagers watching his face on the TV monitors screamed as if on cue. The lyrics and his flailing legs rushed so fast that nobody could keep up with them. He seemed possessed but calm, a wild man who was in absolute control. For the first time on television, Presley looked like a professional singer, an artist who was consciously beginning to shape the style he had been creating.

Presley's "Toast of the Town" appearance caused even more of an uproar among parents than any of his other performances. Letters from all over the nation called Presley's gyrations sinful, scandalous, and shameless. Sullivan responded by ordering his cameramen only to shoot Presley from the waist up during his next appearance. Presley slyly got around such censorship by unleashing his wildest performance yet. He rolled his head, pumped his shoulders suggestively, winked, sneered, and pouted as if in an ecstatic fit. The screams from the studio audience nearly drowned out his singing. For the first time, as cameras scanned the crowd, it was possible to pick out a few glossy pompadours where before all the young men had worn crew cuts. Some daring teens were beginning to dress like their idol.

For his second tune, Presley switched gears effortlessly to sing a quietly moving old-time religious hymn, "Peace in the Valley." This performance was almost as startling as his rock 'n' roll tune. Ministers all over the nation had been calling Presley a terrible sinner for dancing as he sang, yet here he stood stock-still performing a spiritual song with absolute conviction. An instinctive rebel, Presley seemed to be pointing his performance at those ministers, but he also may have been aiming it at the millions of fans he had won in a few short months. It was as if he was saying, "Whether you love me or hate me, don't think you can pigeonhole me as a guy who just shakes his hips. I'm after something bigger than that."

On television in 1956, Elvis Presley introduced the nation to a riveting new kind of music called rock 'n' roll that would gradually spread around the world, revolutionizing its popular culture. But that was not enough for this young visionary. Over the next two decades the world was to discover just how big his ambitions really were.

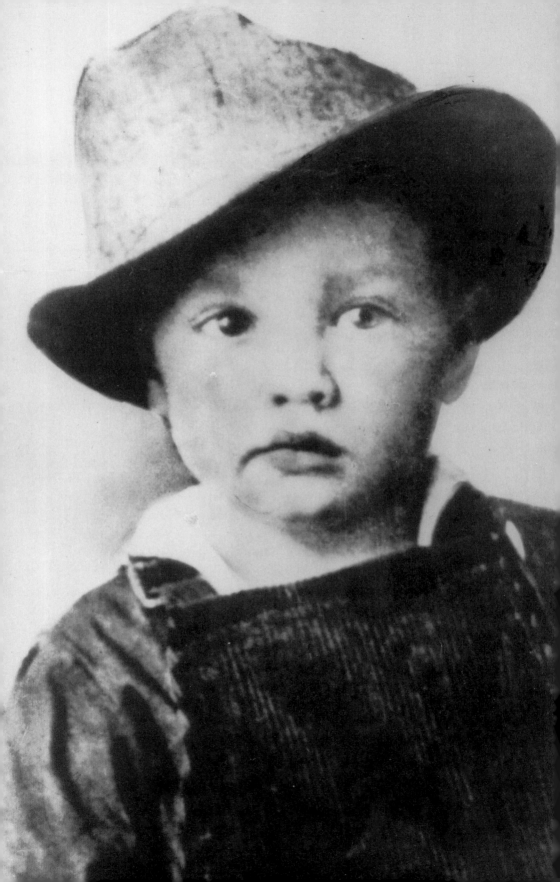

2 ★ Baby Let's Play House

WHEN ELVIS PRESLEY WAS BORN, on Tuesday, January 8, 1935, no one would have guessed that he stood a chance to be famous one day. His poverty-stricken young parents, Vernon and Gladys Presley, had been raised as farmers in northern Mississippi. They had moved only recently into a small house in East Tupelo, a poor section of Tupelo, Mississippi, separated from the rest of town by a levee and a set of railroad tracks. With his own hands, Vernon had built a sturdy two-room home on Old Saltillo Road that included a porch and outhouse. Outside he kept a cow and some chickens. He probably did not expect to own much more than that during his lifetime.

The Presleys' baby was born at the lowest point of the Great Depression, a period when one in three Americans was out of work. In Mississippi, the poorest state in the nation, unemployment was even higher than elsewhere. But Gladys had found a job as a seamstress at the Tupelo Garment Factory, and Vernon worked part-time as a laborer.

In those days, in the rural South, most babies were born at home. A doctor and a midwife assisted when Gladys went into labor, but it was not an easy

At the age of three, Elvis Presley already possessed the languid eyes and pouting mouth that would later become his trademarks as a matinee idol.

birth. She carried twins, and the first was stillborn. The midwife—having no time for mourning—wrapped the dead infant in a blanket, handed the bundle to Vernon Presley, and continued to help his wife give birth to the second twin.

The stress of labor weakened both mother and child, so they were rushed to the hospital, where they recuperated for two weeks. During that time the Presleys named both of their twins. The dead infant's tombstone read "Jesse Garon Presley." His brother was given a rhyming name, Elvis Aaron, in keeping with local tradition. For several years Elvis's family spelled his middle name "Aron," but Elvis later switched to the traditional spelling with two *A*'s. Elvis's first name came from Vernon Presley's middle name; Jesse was named after Vernon's father.

The family never forgot their stillborn son, often wondering aloud about how things would have been different if he had survived. A featured event of young Elvis's birthdays was the annual visit to the cemetery, where the family laid flowers on Jesse's grave. The surviving twin felt the loss of his brother deeply for the rest of his life. As biographer Dave Marsh wrote, "Elvis was fascinated (and terrified) by the thought that he had possessed (and lost) an exact double, perhaps feeling that this was proof that he was special."

Elvis's mother did everything she could to make her sickly infant feel special, too. She quit her job at the garment factory so she could spend every waking moment with her son. Even when she joined her neighbors to pick cotton in the fields late that summer, she propped her infant on her gunnysack and pulled him along the cotton rows as she worked. As one friend remembered, "Gladys was foolish about Elvis—just foolish—she never let that boy out of her sight." Over the years the two developed a bond so close that it almost seemed they could read each other's thoughts. Vernon Presley doted on the boy, too. Like many poverty-stricken couples, the Presleys were determined that their son would have a better way of life than they had.

The attachment between Elvis and his mother was especially close. The death of Elvis's twin made Gladys excessively fearful and protective about Elvis's health. She was never able to have another child, and she focused all of her maternal energy on Elvis. Some relatives have claimed that she doted on Elvis to the exclusion of her husband, who felt left out and spent more and more time away from home. Gladys's obsessive closeness with her son may have been increased by resentment over her husband's failure to hold a steady job.

The Presleys joined the new Assembly of God church down the street as soon as it opened. They both had good

Elvis's mother, Gladys, worked in this factory, the Tupelo Garment Plant, to help provide for her family.

Vernon and Gladys Presley pose with their son, Elvis.

voices, which rang out together during Sunday services, but neither dared to join the church choir. They were shocked one Sunday when Gladys suddenly noticed that her two-year-old toddler had left her side and scrambled up to the choir platform to sing. This was the earliest indication that Elvis Presley had the instincts of a performer.

In East Tupelo during the Great Depression, no one had much, but everybody shared what they had. Despite the hard times they encountered, the Presleys were part of a close-knit extended family and enjoyed the friendship of their neighbors. As Elvis recollected many years later, "There wasn't much money, but there was a lot of love."

When the youngster was just three years old, however, calamity struck. His tenderhearted father was sent to jail. Trying to keep their families fed, Vernon Presley and two friends had sold a hog for $4. Angry at how little money they received for the animal, they made a crucial misstep, altering the check to read $40. At their trial, friends, neighbors, and church members all pleaded with the judge to let the men go, but in the end they were sentenced to three years at hard labor at Parchman Farm State Penitentiary, the most infamous prison in the nation. Chagrined, Vernon bid his pretty wife and their three-year-old son good-bye.

The next year, 1938, was especially hard for the Presleys. Vernon endured backbreaking farm work under the twin terrors of the sweltering subtropical sun and a prison guard's icy stare. Because the Presleys were share-croppers who were allowed to live on their neighbor's land only if they farmed it and gave half the crop to the owner, Gladys had to give up the house her husband had built to move in with the family of her first cousin, Frank Richards, in South Tupelo. Under that arrangement, she could leave Elvis in their care during the day and earn some money washing clothes at Mid-South Laundry. Twice a month a loyal friend drove five hours each way to take Gladys and her son to visit Vernon in prison. Church was the only place Elvis's mother seemed to be able to forget her worries. She and Elvis went to three services a week, singing together and sharing community meals afterward with neighbors.

Gladys Presley fought tirelessly to get her husband out of prison, circulating a petition among her neighbors that pleaded with the Mississippi governor for leniency due to hardship. At last, on February 6, 1939, the governor relented, releasing Vernon and his cohorts after one year in prison. Having lost their home, the family moved briefly to the Mississippi gulf coast, where Vernon found work in a navy shipyard at Pascagoula. Like the other shipfitters' families, they lived in a one-room cabin with walls made of screening. Lonely for their friends in Tupelo, they returned home after eight months, sharing rooms with family members while they looked for a place of their own.

Elvis was six years old when the United States entered World War II in 1941. Vernon's prison record kept him from being drafted for military service. Ironically, he found work helping to build a prison, then took another job in a munitions factory in Memphis, Tennessee, returning home only on weekends. Holding the family together as she always had—by sheer willpower and hard work—Gladys made sure her son was ready for school. In September 1941, she walked him to the modern, well-run East Tupelo Consolidated School on Lake Street, as she would every day for years afterward. Like the other impoverished students of his neighborhood, Elvis delighted at such wonders as radiators, electric lighting, and indoor plumbing, which he had never beheld in his own home.

Gladys Presley had always kept a watchful eye on her only son; some say she smothered him with attention. But once he started school, Elvis began to strike out on his own. An average student, Elvis apparently had only one true love from an early age: music. And he was determined not to save his singing just for church.

Remarkably, by the age of eight, Elvis had already learned to hitchhike five miles to downtown Tupelo on his own. The city's lone radio station, WELO, held a "Saturday Jamboree" program at the courthouse every week. Anyone who wanted to perform could just show up and stand in line. When Elvis's turn first came, he stepped onto a fruit crate in order to reach the microphone, then crooned an old country tune entitled "Old Shep." The song, which could drag on for several minutes, recounted the heartrending tale of a boy's love for his dog.

Prisoners of the Mississippi State Penitentiary, bearing hoes, march off to the cotton fields to perform hard labor. Elvis's father, Vernon, was sent to the penitentiary in 1938 for altering a check.

As Presley biographer Elaine Dundy recounted in *Gladys and Elvis* (1985), garage mechanic and country musician Reggie Bell often picked up Elvis to take him to the jamboree. Afterward, Elvis would sit quietly in the corner of the WELO radio studio while Bell performed with the Lee County Ramblers, a country-and-western band. During their broadcasts Elvis met his first musical hero, the country singer Carvel Lee Ausborn, known as Mississippi Slim. One radio announcer recalled that Elvis "followed Slim around like a pet dog." Elvis even talked the well-known singer into joining him for a Saturday Jamboree performance. Slim humored the youngster, saying afterward, "His timing's all off, but he's doing a good job for an eight year old."

Elvis undertook these expeditions into Tupelo entirely on his own. His doting mother never stopped him, but she also never came to see him perform. Through his own efforts, he began to learn the ways of professional musicians at an early age, broadcasting his voice over the radio throughout his hometown and performing in public without any qualms. Most of Presley's biographers have portrayed him as musically naive. On the contrary, he began to build his musical career before he learned to multiply and divide.

When Elvis was not singing in Tupelo, he spent his free time immersed in comic books or watching movies at the Strand Theatre downtown. He especially liked the comic-book superhero Captain Marvel, Jr., who had a lightning bolt on his costume and wore his glistening black hair with one forelock falling down over his brow. Most of Elvis's friends preferred western movies, but Elvis was dazzled by musicals, entranced by the elegant dancing of Fred Astaire and the effortless singing of Bing Crosby.

At the age of 10, Elvis finally saved enough money from yard work and collecting Coke bottles for their 2¢

deposits to buy a guitar. The child-sized instrument cost $7.75. Elvis's minister, Frank Smith, who played guitar in church, helped him learn a few chords. Family members taught him some more. But his hero Mississippi Slim provided the most consistent tutorials, showing him minor chords, sharps, and flats, and encouraging him to keep practicing. Soon Elvis learned to strum along as he sang for the "Saturday Jamboree."

When Elvis played "Old Shep" for his fifth-grade homeroom teacher Mrs. J. C. Grimes, she could not believe his talent. "He sang it so sweetly, it liked to make me cry," she recalled years later. Mrs. Grimes entered Elvis in the Children's Talent Contest at the upcoming Mississippi-Alabama Fair. At the contest, performing in front of a bandstand that held 2,000 people, the youngster once again sang "Old Shep." He won second prize: five dollars and free admission to all the amusement park rides.

The town of Tupelo, Mississippi, shown here in 1928, was a bustling urban community during Elvis's childhood in the 1930s and 1940s. Elvis's family lived in East Tupelo, a poor section of town separated from the rest of Tupelo by railroad tracks.

33

When World War II ended in 1945, Vernon Presley lost his job at the munitions plant in Memphis. He returned to Tupelo, found work as a truck driver, and tried to buy a house. But the family still could not make ends meet and eventually gave up the house to settle in an old shack on Mulberry Alley near the East Tupelo town dump. They had always been poor, but they had never fallen this low.

The Presleys, as always, relieved their troubles in church, singing together at Sunday services, camp meetings, revivals, and reunions. For Elvis, music seemed to be everywhere. On the radio at home, he listened to country music stars perform at the Grand Ole Opry in Nashville, Tennessee. In church, he learned to play the piano, finding it much easier than the guitar. His choir leaders discovered that even though Elvis could not read sheet music, he had perfect pitch and easily learned to perform hymns by ear. Sometimes the 11-year-old snuck over to the swanky Tupelo Hotel on Spring Street, where he sang for tips, strumming his little guitar.

After the Presleys moved, however, Elvis had to adjust to a change of schools. Arriving barefoot and in overalls, he quickly discovered that he was one of the poorest students at Milam School, which sat in the heart of Tupelo. Most of his classmates ignored him outright; others made him the brunt of their jokes. Always popular before, Elvis was probably confused and hurt by the insults, but every day his mother walked with him right to the school door, making sure he did not turn back.

Fortunately, music came to the rescue. Early in the school year, a teacher asked if anyone would like to perform, and Elvis jumped at the chance. Standing shyly at the chalkboard, he crooned his favorite standby, "Old Shep." The class applauded, and from then on he brought his guitar to school every day. Music did not solve all of his problems, though. One classmate recalled Elvis as "a

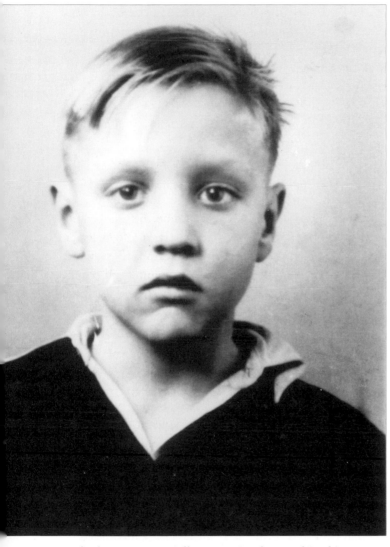

Elvis became interested in music at an early age. He brought his guitar to school with him every day, and on the weekends he sang on radio station WELO's "Saturday Jamboree."

sad, shy, not especially attractive boy, a bit clumsy . . . standing on the stage of the auditorium playing his guitar as part of a talent contest and *not* winning."

Trying to match his classmates' new clothes with his own bravado, Elvis began to say that his ambition was to sing at the Grand Ole Opry, the popular bastion of country music. Most students just smirked. But if they

35

listened to their radios on the weekend, they could sometimes hear Elvis singing on the "Saturday Jamboree" on
WELO. After one performance with his idol Mississippi
Slim, the singer told him, "You're good to be as young as
you are—just keep working."

When Gladys Presley went back to work at the Mid-
South Laundry, the Presleys moved once again, finding
a slightly better apartment on North Green Street. Their
new home was near the middle-class black neighborhood
called Shakerag. The Presleys were poorer than most of
their black neighbors, but their musically inquisitive
son was welcomed to tent services at the Sanctified
Church. Elvis heard a different kind of music there. Black
gospel singers let their voices soar, swoop, and break, as
if they could not contain their religious rapture. Ministers
leaped about the stage, falling to their knees and bursting
into song. There was an unbridled passion in their performances that Elvis had never seen in white churches.

Elvis met guitar players in Shakerag, too. Men who
worked as railroad porters or chefs during the day sat on
their porches in the evening playing unearthly, tinkling
notes and singing sly, guttural songs about the kind of
hard times Elvis's family had seen firsthand. The blond,
blue-eyed white boy had never heard blues before, but he
tried to play along. The musicians humored him, showing him how to use the worn-down neck of a broken
bottle to make his guitar strings wail and moan.

Hungry for music in every form, Elvis soaked up all
the fertile musical influences of northern Mississippi that
he could. He was not alone in these pursuits. Though
largely ignored by the rest of the nation, blues, gospel,
and country music were evolving rapidly in the region.
In towns up and down the Mississippi River, talented
youngsters like Elvis could pick and choose among the
singers and styles they liked the best. When these young
artists—among them Leontyne Price, Miles Davis, B. B.

King, Muddy Waters, Chuck Berry, Fats Domino, and Jerry Lee Lewis—eventually began to make records in the 1940s and 1950s, they combined these styles in revolutionary new ways that changed the face of music forever.

Elvis Presley was perhaps the most ambitious young musician of them all. Since the age of two he had sung several times weekly in church; since the age of eight he had performed at school and on the radio, scrutinizing country musicians at work in the studio and craving the opportunity to join them. At Tupelo's Strand Theatre he had studied the sophisticated movie crooners. He learned to sing and play guitar and piano with gospel, country, and blues inflections, and he even tasted a moment of glory in winning a prize at the Mississippi-Alabama Fair. Biographers like to describe Elvis Presley as an overnight sensation. That may be so, but a lifetime of musical experience preceded that sensational night.

3 In the Ghetto

I N 1948, AT THE AGE OF 13, Elvis Presley's youthful life in small-town Mississippi ended. Fired by the Tupelo trucking company he worked for, Vernon Presley decided to move his family a hundred miles away to Memphis, Tennessee, where he had held a factory job during World War II. As Elvis remembered later, "Dad packed all our belongings in boxes and put them on top and in the trunk of a 1939 Plymouth. We left Tupelo overnight. We were broke, man, broke."

According to Earl Greenwood, Elvis's second cousin, Vernon's decision to move was also prompted by another run-in with the law. Apparently the sheriff had caught Vernon making and selling illegal moonshine whiskey and had told Vernon that he had the choice of returning to jail or leaving town.

The only time Elvis had ever been to Memphis, Tennessee, was on a church outing to the city zoo. The bustling Mississippi River port must have seemed strange, frightening, and intriguing to the youngster, especially during the years when his father had worked there. Having spent his childhood in a sleepy small town of 10,000 people, Elvis would now grow to adulthood

A key ingredient in the development of Elvis's musical style and stage presence was the influence of the black rhythm-and-blues musicians who performed in the nightclubs—and on the street corners— of Memphis's famed Beale Street.

in a sprawling city 30 times the size of Tupelo. From 1948 on, Memphis would always be his home.

Lacking money and jobs, the Presleys could not hope for much of a home at first, and for a time they depended on welfare to make ends meet. They moved from one run-down boardinghouse to another until they landed in a rambling four-storied house at 572 Poplar Avenue, near the downtown business district and in the heart of the city's slums. The old house had been broken up into tiny one-family apartments. As many as 60 people lived in the building at a time. Even when they had lived near the town dump in Tupelo, the Presleys' lodgings had been better than this.

But Gladys Presley resolved to make the best of a bad situation. She quickly found work as a seamstress at Fashion Curtains, enrolled her reluctant son in the small

At age 14, Elvis sits with a companion on the sidewalk of a Memphis street.

neighborhood Christine School, and continued to look for better opportunities. Vernon Presley spent months looking for work, at last settling for a job hauling paint cans for the United Paint Company nearby. When his back began to hurt, he cut back on his hours, relying more and more on his wife's meager salary.

Within a year, Gladys Presley's search for opportunities paid off. She found a rewarding job as a nurse's aid at St. Joseph's Hospital and, shortly thereafter, a better place to live. The family moved to the Lauderdale Courts, a new redbrick federal housing project on Winchester Avenue. Though the project was drab and overcrowded, the Presleys' two-bedroom apartment was cozy. For the first time in his life, Elvis had a room of his own. Following his mother's industrious example, Elvis earned money after school mowing lawns and pumping gas. The family soon joined an Assembly of God church in the neighborhood, attending services every Sunday as they had in Tupelo.

At the age of 14, Elvis started school at the imposing redbrick Humes High School, where he became 1 of 1,600 students. If he had seemed an outcast in Tupelo because of his poverty, at least his music had saved him from complete obscurity. The urbane students at Humes instantly labeled him a rural hick who was beneath their notice entirely. To make matters worse, Elvis's polite manners made him something of a "teacher's pet," so the students despised him even more. And for the first time, Elvis could not rely on his music to win them over. His voice had begun to change, making him afraid to sing for fear of sounding like a frog. Furthermore, as if that were not bad enough, he came down with a florid case of acne.

Elvis hated his first day at school so much that he ran all the way home afterward. He pleaded with his mother not to make him go back. She stroked his sandy hair and told him, as she always had, that even though he came from a poor country family he was just as good as anybody else. In her arms his confidence gradually returned, but just to make sure, Gladys Presley walked all the way to Humes High with her teenage son every day for the rest of the school year.

Somehow the lanky youngster from Tupelo made it through his freshman year at Humes High School. That summer he worked part-time ushering at the Loew's State Theatre, where he was allowed to watch all of the movies for free. He especially loved the Hollywood newcomer Tony Curtis, whose glistening black hairstyle reminded Elvis of his comic-book hero, Captain Marvel, Jr. Soon Elvis began to sport a similar hairstyle, which he would lovingly maintain for the rest of his life. Only a year out of Tupelo, Elvis had already changed a great deal. In an attempt to stand out in his new surroundings, and per-haps to compensate for his rural roots, he not only wore liberal amounts of grease in his hair, but he had dyed it black. A cousin who had also moved to Memphis from Tupelo said that Elvis's hair now looked like a helmet. Even more startling, Elvis had used mascara to darken his blond eyelashes so that they would not clash with his new hair color.

That summer, with some change in his pocket, Elvis daringly begun to explore his new hometown. At night he visited raucous blues clubs on Beale Street, which bordered the toughest black neighborhood in Memphis. A new kind of music that Elvis could not resist had begun to emerge in these clubs. Black singers like Wynonie Harris and Roy Brown had found a way to combine the sophisticated vocal styles of Elvis's favorite movie singers with the danceable rhythms of bluesmen and the sponta-neous evangelical ravings of revival preachers.

The disc jockeys at local WDIA radio, the only sta-tion in the South devoted to black popular singers, called this music "rhythm and blues." With his earnings, Elvis started collecting rhythm-and-blues records, tunes by Fats Domino, Lloyd Price, and Louis Jordan. By the time he finished high school he owned hundreds of vintage singles. He even began to dress like the flashier patrons of the blues clubs, buying outrageously colored flared, pegged, and patterned outfits from used clothing stores—after spending hours staring at the marvelously garish clothes in Lansky's Clothing Store on Beale Street. Years later, when he could afford all the clothes he wanted, he often returned to Lansky's to shop.

Elvis must have stunned his classmates when he returned to school that fall. The 16-year-old's acne had cleared up, and he had begun to grow handsome, developing the smoldering good looks that would eventually help make him one of the most photographed people on the planet. But his Tony Curtis haircut and his hot pink slacks with black piping were more than the city boys could stand. As Elvis remembered years later, "I had pretty long hair for that time and I tell you it got pretty

Elvis spent his high school years at Humes High School in Memphis. From a poorer and more rural background than most of his classmates, Elvis remained an outsider there.

weird. They used to see me coming down the street and they'd say, 'Hot dang, let's get him, he's a squirrel, he's a squirrel, get him, he just come down outta the trees.'" Every day the other boys taunted and pushed him. At night he awoke from awful nightmares in which he fought to get away from an angry mob.

At last Elvis's nightmare came true. Members of the football team caught the outcast combing his pomaded hair in the boy's room, shoved him against the wall, and pulled out knives in order to shave him. At that point a burly teammate named Red West barged in, shouting, "There ain't no need for this. If he likes his hair that way, well, no sense in hassling him. Now, if you cut his hair, you're gonna have to cut my hair, too; and that's gonna develop into something else." Wary of fighting their teammate, the bullies backed away, mumbling.

Red West became Elvis's first friend in Memphis. His second was the class president, George Klein. The only thing the trio had in common was that they came from poor families, but at Humes High School that was enough. West and Klein did their best to make Elvis feel at home. West convinced him to try out for the football team, and Klein introduced him to the student clubs. Elvis was too small then, at 5 feet 6 inches, to make the football squad—and his overprotective mother was horrified at the thought of her only son being injured on the football field. But by the time he graduated from Humes, he had joined the Reserve Officers' Training Corps (ROTC) and clubs in biology, English, speech, and history.

Elvis began to regain his singing voice, too. Playing his guitar in the courtyard at home, he discovered that he could sing better than ever, eventually spanning three octaves. In the evening, neighbors gathered in the courtyard to listen to the youngster. Among them was bass player Bill "Blackie" Black, who often visited his aging

A teenage Elvis, showing a hint of a mustache, pauses in a parking lot in Memphis.

mother at the Lauderdale Courts. Black performed with a country band called Doug Poindexter's Starlite Wranglers, whose lead guitarist was Scotty Moore. In just three years Black and Moore would form the core of Presley's revolutionary new band.

Black liked the young singer and often took out his upright bass to play along on renditions of contemporary country songs. Sometimes they practiced one song together for four hours until they got it exactly right. Black told Elvis that an electrician named Sam Phillips had just opened a new recording studio downtown. For just four dollars anyone could stop in and make a record. Black encouraged Elvis to do that. Who could tell, maybe Phillips would like what he heard and sign him up? Elvis grinned sheepishly at the suggestion, saying he did not feel ready to risk an audition just yet. But from that day forth, making a record for Sam Phillips became one of his keenest dreams.

Nurturing that dream, Elvis began to frequent nightclubs more than ever, sometimes sweeping up, cleaning the kitchen, or working as a carhop on weekends. Between sets, on occasion, the performers would allow him to sneak onstage to sing a few songs. Reportedly, he even dared once to sing at an otherwise all-black amateur contest at the Palace Theatre downtown.

As much as Elvis enjoyed rhythm-and-blues music, he still loved gospel singing more than anything else. Memphis at that time was a hotbed of energetic, showy white gospel performances, and Elvis often attended all-night sings at Ellis Auditorium, where he marveled at the dynamic harmonies of groups such as the Blackwoods and the Songfellows. Elvis admired the Statesmen Quartet most of all. Years later he would call their lead singer, Jake Hess, his greatest musical influence. Never one to let skin color stand in his way, Elvis also attended black gospel sings conducted by a local preacher and composer, the Reverend H. W. Brewster. Again, the teenager must have cut an odd figure in the audience, dressed like a flashy punk but waving his hands and singing at the top of his lungs about the glory of God.

If Elvis's nights were filled with music, he made sure his days were, too. During his free time, when he was not listening to WDIA on the radio or wearing out his ever-expanding record collection, he walked the streets of Memphis with his old guitar, singing for anyone who would stop and listen. Singer Johnny Burnette remembers Elvis performing at fire stations, because he knew that firemen had more free time to listen than other folks.

When Elvis turned 18, though, he recognized that it was time to set aside idle pastimes and seriously plan his future. His family had just left the projects, moving across the street to a private apartment at 462 Alabama Avenue. More than anything, Elvis wanted to find a good job so his mother could stop working. He pleaded with her to let him drop out of school, as most of his poorer class-mates had already done. Though Vernon Presley——still nursing his bad back—agreed, Gladys would have none of it. Mr. Presley was by some accounts more than willing to concede the role of family breadwinner to his son. The amiable but unambitious Vernon rarely had a full-time job, and when he had one he usually quit, complaining of a bad back.

But Gladys Presley was adamant that her son graduate from high school. At the age of 39, she rode a bus to Tupelo to pick cotton that fall, just so her son could stay in school. Though Elvis worked evenings, she made him quit when she heard that he had begun to fall asleep during class.

With such strong backing from his mother, Elvis slogged through his senior year, majoring in English (his favorite class), history, and shop. Most of his classmates still ignored him. One remembered later that "he had no personality, if you know what I mean. Just acted kind of goofy, sitting in the back of the class, playing his guitar. No one knew that he was ever going to be *any*thing."

That idea began to change, however, when Elvis per-formed at the annual Humes High Variety Show. Elvis stood out among 29 other acts, wearing a red cowboy shirt and singing a plaintive country tune, "Cold, Cold Icy Fingers." Students who had been prepared to heckle their hillbilly classmate were moved to tears by his soulful performance, and their applause easily made him the winner of the contest. For his encore Elvis sang his perennial standby "Old Shep." Stunned by the cheers of classmates who had previously ignored him, he ran back-stage afterward, repeating, "They really liked me, they really liked me," as if he could not believe it.

Years later Elvis recalled, "It was amazing how popular I was in school after that." For the first time girls invited him to parties—if he promised to bring his guitar. There was no danger that he would forget it; he brought it to school every day.

With graduation approaching, Elvis made plans to get a job on the assembly line at the Precision Tool Company. College was out of the question for a poor, non-athletic boy who had been only an average student. But before settling down to a lifetime of drudgery, Elvis suddenly disappeared one week before school was out.

This excerpt from the yearbook of one of his classmates bears Elvis's signature and the dedication, "Best luck to a swell guy—Elvis."

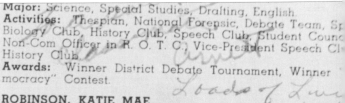

Major: Science, Special Studies, Drafting, English.
Activities: Thespian, National Forensic, Debate Team, Sp Biology Club, History Club, Speech Club, Student Counc Non-Com Officer in R. O. T. C., Vice-President Speech Cl History Club.
Awards: Winner District Debate Tournament, Winner mocracy" Contest.

ROBINSON, KATIE MAE
Major: Commercial, Home Ec., English.
Activities: F. H. A., History Club, English Club, Vice-Club.

RULEMAN, SHIRLEY

Major: Home Ec., Commercial, English.
Activities: National Honor Society, F. H. A., Y-Teens Cheerleader, Sabre Club, History Club, English Club, Fin R. O. T. C., President Home Ec. Class.

PRESLEY, ELVIS ARON

Major: Shop, History, English.
Activities: R. O. T. C., Biology Club, English Club, Hist Club.

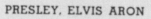

PERRY, ROBERT EARL

Major: History, Science, English.
Activities: Biology Club, T&I Club, Key Club, Baseba President Key Club, Boys' Vice-President Senior Class, Pr
Awards: All-Star American Legion Baseball Team 1952 Society.

SANDERS, MARY LOUISE

Carrying just 10 cents in his pocket, he hitchhiked 240 miles to Meridian, Mississippi, for the chance to perform at a music festival in honor of the great country singer Jimmie Rodgers, who had been born there. Elvis won second prize—a new guitar—then hitchhiked home and graduated with a testimonial of good conduct the next week. By performing well at this contest, Elvis proved to himself that his musical ambitions were not entirely ridiculous. He would get a job, but nothing would stop him from dreaming about a musical career.

Elvis hated assembly line work. He stayed at the Precision Tool Company for just three weeks before finding a truck-driving job with Crown Electric Company. Like most teenage boys of the time, Elvis loved cars and the romance of the highways. He soon added long sideburns, like the ones long-distance truckers wore, to his usual Tony Curtis pompadour.

After work, as always, the young trucker tirelessly roamed the nightclub circuit, sometimes traveling all the way across the state for the chance to perform. Roy Hall, a Nashville club owner, hired him and fired him in one night, explaining later, "He weren't no damn good." Elvis's rhythm-and-blues hero Roy Brown remembers him sneaking onstage between sets at a concert in Tupelo: "He was up there playing and singing, nobody paying any attention to him." Sometimes Elvis sang at a suburban Memphis nightclub called the Eagle's Nest. Dressed in flashy hipster attire, he attempted popular tunes by the crooner Dean Martin, while the main performers—a country swing band—took a break.

Every day, it seemed, Elvis drove his truck past Sun Studio at 706 Union Avenue. The sign over the door read: The Memphis Recording Service—Combining the Newest and Best Equipment. This was radio announcer Sam Phillips's studio, where Elvis's friend Bill Black had encouraged him to make a record. Elvis knew that pre-

Before he became a professional singer, Elvis paid four dollars to make a recording of himself singing "My Happiness" and "That's When Your Heartaches Begin," which had been hits for the Ink Spots, shown here. Elvis made the single acetate disc because, he said, "I had a notion to find out what I really sounded like."

viously unknown blues singers such as B. B. King, Howlin' Wolf, and Junior Parker had started their recording careers at Sun. Black had told him that Phillips was beginning to record country singers, too. But what Phillips really wanted was a singer who could combine the blues and country sound, tapping into black audiences and white audiences alike. Black thought Elvis might fit the bill.

Elvis drove his truck past Sun Studio for a year before finally summoning the courage to go inside. As he later remembered it, "I went to Sun, paid my four bucks to the lady because I had a notion to find out what I really sounded like. I had been singing all my life and I was kind of curious." Of course, there was more to it than that.

Elvis must have seen this as his big chance. But in the waiting room he sat among a dozen other teenagers with guitars, wearing their best cowboy shirts and dreaming of impressing Sam Phillips.

It must have come as both a disappointment and a relief to discover that Phillips was not in the studio that day. His assistant, Marion Keisker, a local radio personality, was in charge instead. Like Elvis's high school teachers, she grew intrigued by the shy boy in the outrageous clothes, asking, "What kind of singer are you?"

The boy who had grown up singing gospel, country, blues, and movie tunes answered obligingly, "I sing all kinds."

Smiling politely at that, Keisker then asked, "Who do you sound like?"

With shy pride, he mumbled, "I don't sound like nobody."

When Elvis's turn came to record, he crooned two songs by the popular black quartet the Ink Spots, "My Happiness" and "That's When Your Heartaches Begin." The Ink Spots sounded a lot like the gospel groups Elvis enjoyed at Ellis Auditorium, and he easily mimicked their style. Impressed, Keisker began to make a tape recording for Phillips halfway through the song. As she recalled, "I got maybe the last third of the first song and all of the second. I don't even know if Elvis knew that I was taping it."

Elvis left the studio wondering if he had made any kind of impression. He took the four-dollar acetate record home and played it for his proud mother, complaining that his guitar sounded "like somebody beating on a bucket lid." Back at Sun Studio, Marion Keisker carefully boxed the tape recording of his performance. On the box she wrote his name and address, with the note: "Good ballad singer—hold."

4 ★ The Rising Sun

NOTHING CAME OF Elvis Presley's first stab at a recording career. Sun Studio owner Sam Phillips apparently listened to his tape and just shrugged. So Elvis continued to drive a truck during the day and visit his usual musical haunts at night, biding his time for another try at fame. In the meantime, he fell in love.

Dixie Locke was 15, three years younger than her teenage suitor. They met at church. To Elvis she was "kind of small with long, dark hair that came down to her shoulders and the biggest smile I've ever seen anywhere. She was always laughing, always enjoying herself." The couple drove around Memphis after-hours in the Crown Electric Company delivery truck, swimming at the lake or sharing ice cream sodas at the drug store. Dixie surprised Elvis by taking his dreams and ambitions seriously. He was amazed to discover that she was just as easy to talk to as his mother.

With Dixie's encouragement, Elvis went back to Sun Studio four days before his 19th birthday. This time he recorded two country songs, "Casual Love Affair" and "I'll Never Stand in Your Way." And this time Sam Phillips

Elvis signs autographs for a mob of admirers. Just a year and a half after he cut his first record at Sun Studio in July 1954, he was performing on national television.

manned the recording equipment. But he did not seem especially impressed, writing down the young singer's address and sending him on his way. Stepping up his efforts at building a singing career, Elvis then auditioned for his favorite gospel group, the Songfellows. They turned him down, saying his versatile voice did not quite fit their quartet sound. Elvis went back to Dixie dejected. Throughout the spring of 1954 he tried to come to grips with the realization that he might be a truck driver for the rest of his life. He swore that if he ever got another chance at a singing career, nothing would stand in his way.

That chance came in May, when Sam Phillips called, offering him a chance to audition for a new song,

This extremely rare photograph shows Elvis in 1954, just before his career took off. The budding singer was still employed at the time as a truck driver for Crown Electric Company.

"Without You." Elvis ran all the way to the studio, bursting in the door, panting, almost before the phone line went dead. Here was the opportunity he had waited for! But no matter how many times he tried, he could not make "Without You" work.

Phillips liked his determination, though, and thought there was something interesting in the way Elvis tried to add all sorts of odd inflections into each line. It was as if he had so much to say that no single song could hold all of his feelings. Finally, Phillips gave up on "Without You" and asked Presley to sing everything he knew. Late into the night Phillips and his assistant Marion Keisker listened to the young man pour his heart into gospel, blues, country, and movie-musical tunes.

As Phillips listened, he decided to have Elvis rehearse the following week with one of his studio guitarists, Scotty Moore. Maybe together they could come up with a saleable sound. Elvis dressed for the rehearsal in his showiest outfit, hot pink shirt and slacks with white buck shoes. Moore later recalled, "I thought my wife was going to run out the back door, people just didn't dress like that at the time." Trying to suppress a smile, Moore said, "Elvis Presley, huh? That name sounds like something out of science fiction!" Elvis laughed good-naturedly, and then they got down to work.

Soon Elvis's old friend, bass player Bill Black, joined the rehearsal sessions. He and Moore had played together for years and had been looking for a singer to back. The two older musicians were used to staid country performers, but Phillips encouraged them to let the kid try out anything he liked. They rehearsed a ridiculously wide range of tunes by singers as diverse as Hank Williams, Billy Eckstine, Hank Snow, and Dean Martin.

After two months of rehearsals, the musicians got together at Sun Studio on July 5 to show Sam Phillips what they had come up with. For the audition they stuck

Elvis poses with Sam Phillips, the owner of the now-legendary Sun Studio in Memphis, Tennessee. Phillips launched Presley's recording career in 1954 with the single "That's All Right (Mama)" on the Sun label.

to country songs, disappointing Phillips, who had hoped to hear a distinctive new style of some sort. Then during a rest break, Elvis picked up his guitar and launched into a blues song, "That's All Right (Mama)." Moore and Black joined in, rushing the beat as Elvis's voice skipped through the verses. "What was that?" Phillips asked from the control room. They all just shrugged. Afraid to trust his ears, Phillips turned on the tape machine and told them, "Whatever it was, I want you to do it again. Just like that, don't mess with it. Keep it simple."

At last Sam Phillips had found the sound he was looking for, a magical combination of country-and-western, blues, and gospel styles. Somehow it all seemed deceptively simple. Moore's light-fingered electric guitar licks, Black's bass racing like a speeding heartbeat, and Presley's drumsticks tapping together like nervous fingers snapping while he cut loose with fluid vocal spontaneity all added up to an exhilarating sound full of verve and sly wit. Because there were no drums to anchor the rhythm, the music skipped along, as airy and confident as Presley's voice. Here was something new indeed. Phillips did not tamper much with the sound, adding only an embellishment he called slapback, a quavering echo that made Elvis's voice seem to shimmer. Scores of producers have sought to mimic that technique ever since.

The next evening the trio recorded an old country tune, "Blue Moon of Kentucky," again cannily speeding up the beat to complement Presley's exuberant vocals. Phillips took his only copy of those songs to his friend, Memphis disc jockey Dewey Phillips at WHBQ radio, the same day. Presley knew that his songs would play on the radio that night, but he was too nervous to wait around to hear them. He went to his neighborhood movie theater alone and sat in the dark chewing his fingernails.

At home, Gladys Presley could hardly believe her ears. She told a friend that the most amazing thing was "hearing them say his name over the radio just before they put on that record. That shook me so it stayed with me right through the whole song—Elvis Presley—just my son's name. I couldn't rightly hear the record the first time around."

Fortunately, Gladys had many more opportunities. At WHBQ the switchboard lit up with calls, so Phillips had to play both sides 14 times in a row. Then he called the Presley home, trying to find the singer for an interview. The proud parents raced over to the movie house and found their son in the dark. "What's happened, Mama?" he sheepishly asked. "Nothing but good, son," she replied.

Radio listeners were excited to hear that a local boy, a 19-year-old Humes High School graduate, had recorded these wild new songs. Seven thousand requests for the record came in to the studio before the interview ended. Sam Phillips rushed the songs into the stores within a couple of weeks, and by the end of the month "That's All Right (Mama)" had reached the number three spot on the Memphis country-and-western charts, with orders from as far away as Dallas and Atlanta.

On July 30, 1954, Elvis Presley, Scotty Moore, and Bill Black played their first live concert at the outdoor Overton Park Bandshell. Presley recalled the appearance this way:

> I was scared stiff. I came out, and I was doing a fast-type tune, and everybody was hollering, and I didn't know what they were hollering at. Everybody was screaming and everything, and I came offstage and they told me that they was hollering because I was wiggling. And so I went back out for an encore, and I did a little more. And the more I did, the wilder they went.

Presley had seen rhythm-and-blues performers such as Wynonie Harris and Ukelele Ike "wiggle" while singing on Beale Street. Black gospel singers often seemed possessed by the spirit, dancing and shaking across the stage. But white country-and-western performers stayed put while they sang, at least until Elvis Presley came along. By adding a black performing style to his onstage presentation, Presley had once again combined his musical influences, providing a perfect complement to his singing style. His fans may not have understood what he was up to, but they loved him just the same.

For the rest of the summer, Presley, Moore, and Black performed every weekend. They called themselves The Hillbilly Cat and the Blue Moon Boys, and their music grew tighter and more thrilling the more they practiced. On September 23 they cut their second record, the bluesy "Good Rockin' Tonight," which had already been a hit for Presley's hero Wynonie Harris. On the flip side was the sly, countryish "I Don't Care if the Sun Don't Shine." This record sold 4,000 copies in Memphis in just two weeks.

Scotty Moore (left) backs up a typically unrestrained Elvis Presley. Elvis's uninhibited movements onstage led one reporter to write that viewing him was "like watching a striptease and a malted milk machine at the same time." Another writer compared Presley to "a lovesick outboard motor."

With that success, Presley won the opportunity to fulfill a lifelong dream: to perform at the Grand Ole Opry in Nashville, Tennessee, the home of country-and-western music. But the conservative Opry audience disliked Moore's newfangled electric guitar, Presley's bluesy inflections, and most of all his hip shaking. They all but booed Presley off the stage. Bouncing back from that failure, the next month Presley and his band drove to Shreveport, Louisiana, to perform at the Louisiana Hayride, a more adventurous country music venue that broadcast performances all over the South.

The Hayride audiences quickly became Presley's biggest fans. In November, when the band signed a contract to perform on the Hayride broadcasts every weekend for a year, Presley finally felt confident enough about his singing career to quit his job as a truck driver. Now he was free to travel all over the South, performing practically every night. The combo hired a manager, local radio personality Bob Neal, and added a drummer, D. J. Fontana. Presley's old high school friend and protector, Red West, signed on as an extra driver and bodyguard. For the next year that crew raced from show to show, wearing out one car after another on the backroads of the southern states. The band once estimated that they covered more than 100,000 miles during that first year of touring.

As word spread about Presley, more and more teenage girls began to crowd into the audience, screaming wildly at each of Presley's teasing hip shakes. In Jacksonville, Florida, in May 1955, the singer made the mistake of jokingly inviting all the girls backstage after the show. Hundreds of girls overpowered the police guards and ripped Elvis's clothes off him, tearing them to shreds before his eyes. When the police finally were able to get the singer into his car, they found the vehicle completely covered with names and phone numbers that had been scratched on it or had been written in lipstick.

When Gladys Presley came to watch Elvis perform in a high school gym in Mississippi she was so upset by the wild, grasping fans that she leaped onstage to pull her son away from them. "Why are you trying to kill my boy?" she demanded of one young woman.

"I'm not trying to kill him. I just love him so, I want to touch him," she explained.

Elvis's reaction was more accommodating than his mother's. "Shucks, they were only tearing my clothes. I didn't mind a bit," he said. "I told her, 'Mama, if you're going to feel that way, you'd better not come along to my shows because that stuff is going to keep right on happening'—I hope."

Meanwhile, Sam Phillips continued to market Presley's records, issuing new singles in January, April, and August 1955. As with the other records, Phillips placed a rhythm-and-blues song on one side and a country-and-western tune on the other, hoping to win airplay on black radio stations and white stations alike. Phillips had his biggest success with a song called "Baby, Let's Play House." This sexy blues tune was Presley's first song to make national radio playlists, reaching number 10 on the country-and-western chart.

At last Presley had the money to make things better for his parents. He rented them a nicer home on Lamar Avenue, and then a bigger one on Getwell Street, filling the rooms with kitchen appliances, decorations, and new furniture. He even bought his mother a pink Ford sedan. But as his touring schedule grew ever more busy, he found himself at home less and less. Eventually his girlfriend, Dixie Locke, got tired of waiting for him and announced her engagement to another man. Elvis hated to see Dixie go, but for him there was no turning back now. He had dreamed of a singing career his whole life, and he would do whatever it took to make it work.

In a very short period of time his band had won over thousands of music fans in the southern states. Billed as a "new kind of country-and-western singer," Presley saw

Elvis keeps time on the back of his guitar during a recording session in his breakthrough year of 1956.

his record sales continue to grow throughout 1955. But he instinctively understood that constant touring alone would not win him the nationwide success that he dreamed of. He needed a manager who knew how to get him a big recording contract, widespread exposure, and television appearances. In the spring of 1955 he met such a man, Colonel Tom Parker.

Not only was Parker not a real colonel, his name was not really Tom Parker. Born Andreas Cornelius van

Kuijk in Holland, Parker was living illegally in the United States under an assumed name. His past experiences included a stretch as dogcatcher for the city of Tampa, Florida. There the enterprising schemer had charged local residents $100 to bury their pets, complete with an elaborate funeral, in a cemetery he had created by clearing the trash out of the pound's backyard.

Parker had spent eight or nine years perfecting his skills as a huckster by working with a series of shady

Elvis Presley confers with Colonel Tom Parker in 1956, the year Presley signed a management contract with Parker that gave the Colonel 25 percent of Presley's earnings. Parker's share was increased to an incredible 50 percent in 1967. The day after Presley died, the insatiable Colonel would cut a deal giving himself 75 percent of the income generated by Elvis memorabilia.

traveling carnivals, so successfully adopting a down-home, southern image that in 1948 he was given the honorary title of Colonel by Governor Jimmy "Pappy" Davis of Louisiana. By then he had become a successful manager whose biggest musical clients before landing Elvis had been country singers Eddie Arnold and Hank Snow. At the time Parker met Elvis, the crass and obnoxious ex-carny man had already been fired by the conservative Arnold.

The popular country singer Snow had his own extremely successful multiact traveling roadshow, Hank Snow Jamboree Attractions, which Parker used to lure the Presleys into letting him sign their underage son. Though he dressed like a tacky used car salesman in T-shirts and baggy slacks, Parker knew how to ingratiate himself with the Presleys, telling them, "Now your son just has a million dollars worth of talent. With me he'll have a million dollars."

On August 15, Parker and Presley signed an extraordinary management contract, which did not contain an expiration date but did guarantee that Parker would have the power to negotiate all future contracts, thus giving him complete control over Presley's career. That done, the Colonel went to work.

Very quickly he negotiated a lucrative recording deal with RCA Records in which Sam Phillips gave up the rights to all of Presley's Sun Studio songs for $35,000. (These tunes have since earned RCA millions of dollars.) Another remarkable feature of the deal with RCA was that there was no mention of Hank Snow in the contract. Just three months after Snow had helped Parker reel in Elvis, the Colonel had double-crossed him, ridding himself of his partner for good.

Parker also got the music publishing company Hill & Range to agree to a deal in which Presley was given half of the songwriting credit for every song he recorded, thus doubling his royalties. Parker then traveled to New York to arrange television appearances for his new client, and he even hinted of a movie career for his budding star.

In one short year Presley had realized his dream, moving from truck driving to professional singing. Presley's band played an exciting new style of music that did not even have a name yet. Black people and white people alike bought his records. All over the South teenage girls screamed wildly as he performed. But even he could not have imagined what the next year would bring.

Special Issue On ELVIS PRESLEY

HEP CATS Review

february
25¢

movie scenes from
"LOVE ME TENDER"

dig the new
PAT BOONE

complete story on
ELVIS PRESLEY

no. 1 disk-jockey
ALAN FREED

Exclusive Photos -- Intimate Secrets
FULL PAGES OF PICTURES SUITABLE FOR FRAMING

5 Good Rockin' Tonight

NINETEEN-FIFTY-SIX was the year that rock 'n' roll music exploded across the nation. It was also the year that Elvis Presley became rock 'n' roll's undisputed king. There have been hundreds of overnight sensations in the music business, but no one has ever ridden a rocket to stardom as quickly or as powerfully as Elvis Presley did that year.

On January 8, 1956, Elvis's 21st birthday, Colonel Tom Parker drafted a new management contract granting himself 25 percent of Presley's earnings and making himself Presley's sole "adviser, personal representative and manager." Two days later, Presley's band recorded their major label debut, a gloomy ballad entitled "Heartbreak Hotel." RCA brought in additional musicians for the session, including pianist Floyd Cramer, rhythm guitarist Chet Atkins, and the gospel quartet the Jordanaires, but Presley sounded just as authentic and youthful as he did on the Sun Studio recordings. In a mumbled voice filled with starts, stops, and catches he sang the despairing lyrics.

Elvis's sudden emergence into mass stardom created an incredible demand for Elvis memorabilia. This special issue of the *Hep Cat's Review* was devoted entirely to Elvis and contained dozens of pictures "suitable for framing."

The song perfectly captured an intense melancholy that teenagers found especially compelling. It was released the same week that Presley gave his first television performance on the Dorseys' "Stage Show." The combination of hearing the singer's tortured singing style and watching his nervy dance moves caused an overnight sensation among the nation's youth. The tune hit the national pop charts by March, and with each of Presley's TV appearances its popularity grew. By May, after six TV

Elvis performs with the members of his band. Guitarist Scotty Moore and bassist Bill Black, his first musical collaborators at Sun Studio, played a key role in the creation of Elvis's sound.

appearances on "Stage Show," "Heartbreak Hotel" had become the number one song in the nation.

In March, RCA released the singer's first album, *Elvis Presley*, combining songs recorded at the "Heartbreak Hotel" sessions with unreleased tunes recorded at Sun Studio. One of the most beautiful of these songs, never released as a single, is a Sun Studio ballad, "Blue Moon," which showcases Presley's chilling, ethereal vocal. Though the album hewed closely to the Sun Studio style, during the rest of that year, Presley's band began to build a harder, more rhythmic attack.

At this time similar bands were beginning to break through on the nation's radios. Chuck Berry's stinging guitar solos, Bo Diddley's relentless beat, Little Richard's outrageous squeals of delight, and Bill Haley's enthusiastic call to "Rock Around the Clock" all added up to a new kind of music that Cleveland disc jockey Alan Freed had dubbed "rock 'n' roll." Elvis Presley's recording of "Hound Dog" and his favorite early tune, "Don't Be Cruel," effortlessly summed up the energy, rebelliousness, and fun of this new music. These songs were more raucous than his Sun Studio recordings. The drums and bass traded loud and chaotic rhythms, the guitarist played supple, biting solos, and the singer raced through a dozen vocal tics, yelps, and moans in as many seconds. The tireless Presley sometimes drove his band on to perform as many as 60 takes of a song to capture just the right feeling. It was worth the hard work. The music Presley's band recorded in 1956 is considered by many to be the blueprint for all of the rock 'n' roll that followed.

In one of these recording sessions, Presley also took the opportunity to record the song he had performed live for the first time as an eight-year-old. On his second album, *Elvis,* he sang "Old Shep" with heartfelt conviction, accompanying himself on piano.

Meanwhile, Presley's scorching band continued to tour the nation at a breakneck pace. In the South their teenage fans raved as they always had, but elsewhere the reception was not always so friendly. In April, Colonel Parker booked Presley for a two-week engagement at the New Frontier Hotel in Las Vegas, Nevada, with an audience made up entirely of adults. One local newspaper reported derisively the next day, "Elvis was somewhat like a jug of corn liquor at a champagne party. His body movements were embarrassingly direct. Most of the high rollers breathed a sigh of relief when his set ended."

Colonel Parker made up for his misjudgment in Las Vegas by winning Presley a movie screen test the same month. In a room surrounded by Hollywood bigwigs, Presley and veteran character actor Frank Faylen read lines from a new movie, *The Rainmaker.* Producer Hal Wallis watched with interest. He had seen Presley's TV performances and had read about the way teenage girls swarmed to his concerts, and he believed Presley had the

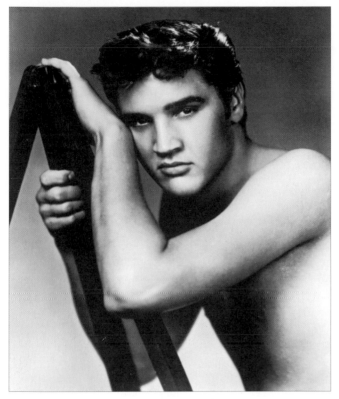

Elvis's sultry good looks made the sexy singer a natural choice for movie roles. Presley would perform in a total of 33 films during his career.

makings of a movie star. When the audition ended, he stood up and offered the singer a lucrative three-movie contract.

Presley could hardly believe his good fortune. All his life he had idolized movie stars like Fred Astaire and Gene Kelly. Some of his stage moves emulated the new screen heroes James Dean and Marlon Brando. As he told a reporter, "Singers come and go, but if you're a good actor, you can last a long time."

Hal Wallis wasted no time in finding a movie for Presley to star in. He chose a Civil War melodrama entitled *The Reno Brothers,* then changed the title to *Love Me Tender* when Presley's song of that name hit radio playlists over the summer. In the movie Presley sings the tune to his leading lady, Debra Paget. When his character dies after a fight, the film ends with his lilting reprise of the song while mourners leave the cemetery after his burial.

Presley had never taken an acting class, of course, but he bluffed his way through the film with his usual good humor. His costar, Richard Egan, remarked, "That boy could charm the birds from the trees. He was so eager and humble, we went out of our way to help him." At first Presley was dazzled to find himself at Hollywood parties with young stars such as Natalie Wood and Sal Mineo, but he relaxed when he found that these stars were equally dazzled to have him in their midst. Before Presley left Hollywood that summer, he and Wood were dating, and he promised to bring her home to meet his parents before the year was out.

Elvis's fans block traffic on Broadway in New York City before the opening of his first movie, *Love Me Tender,* on November 15, 1956.

That home was a brand new ranch-style house that Presley had bought for his parents on Memphis's ex-

clusive Audubon Drive. They had outfitted it with an assortment of colorful furniture and accessories, including a red plastic telephone studded with rhinestones. Having been apart from him for nearly the whole year of his rise to fame, they must have been shocked to see their son step down from an airplane on October 31, 1956, with the beautiful young Hollywood star Natalie Wood on his arm.

Gladys Presley looked past all the trappings of success and read the toll a year of hard work had taken on her son. She had never seen him so pale, and he had thick black semicircles under his eyes. In his new bedroom, decorated at his request with pink wallpaper and a matching bedspread, the king of rock 'n' roll would sleep all day. So many of his fans were waiting for him outside the house that it would have been pointless for him to attempt to go out anyway. Restless again at sunset, he would jump in the pink Cadillac he had recently purchased and be gone with his friends until the sun rose.

Gladys had read about her son's collapse after a concert in Jacksonville, Florida, in August, just two months before. This was the town where Elvis's fans had rioted the previous year. To prevent another outburst, the police had forbidden Presley from shaking his hips during his concert. Slyly, the king of rock 'n' roll had stood stock-still onstage, simply wiggling his pinky finger as he sang. That was all it took to drive the crowd into a frenzy. Once again, he had to escape the crush of adoring fans under police escort. After the last show he had been taken to a hospital suffering from nervous exhaustion, but by the next morning he was back at the hotel, complaining that he could not get any rest in the hospital because the nurses were fighting over him.

In exasperation, Gladys Presley told her son, "If you don't slow down, you won't live past 30." Elvis kissed her on the forehead and laughed, but agreed that he had never been so tired in his life. Natalie Wood stayed in Memphis for only a week. Then she returned to Hollywood, telling the nosy tabloid reporters, "The romance isn't serious." Presley remained at home while he waited for the film *Love Me Tender* to open. In New York City, on November 15, thousands of young people blocked traffic on Broadway to await the unveiling of a 30-foot cutout of their idol, squealing in ecstasy as Presley's face came into view above the movie marquee. Countless fans like these made the movie an instant hit nationwide.

During his stay in Memphis Presley stopped in often at Sun Studio. Sam Phillips was busy working with new stars who had followed in Presley's wake, singers such as Jerry Lee Lewis, Carl Perkins, Roy Orbison, and Johnny Cash. Each of these musicians would become famous as rock 'n' roll took over the radio waves during the next few years. Phillips called their outrageous blend of blues and country music "rockabilly."

A unique recording entitled *Elvis Presley: The Million Dollar Quartet* captured Elvis in an informal jam session with Jerry Lee Lewis, Carl Perkins, and Johnny Cash. Elvis played piano while the four sang gospel, blues, and pop songs, often harmonizing in the church-style quartet mode that Presley loved so much. The recording, released many years afterward, not only juxtaposes four of popular music's all-time greats, but provides a revealing glimpse at how the roots of rock music emerged quite literally from gospel, blues, and country music.

The Presleys enjoyed Christmas at home in 1956 with a brand new white nylon Christmas tree. In one short year their son had brought them treasures—a home, a Cadillac, a roomful of gifts—that they had only dreamed of before. Best of all, Elvis was at last able to assure his mother that she would never have to work again. Wearing a Santa cap and a colorful frock, Gladys danced around the tree with Elvis. The newly wealthy family stood at their new piano and sang gospel songs together as they had always done. It was a fairy tale ending to an astounding year.

If rock 'n' roll stormed the nation in 1956, it completely overwhelmed all other forms of popular music in 1957. Adults who had considered rock 'n' roll a juvenile fad were forced to consider that the music might be around for awhile. British critic Thomas P. Ronan voiced the concerns of the many anxious adults who were wondering what had happened to their children: "Does the music madden them? Does it appeal to some latent jungle strain? Is it an outlet for the frustrations and insecurities that seem to afflict teen-agers?"

Whatever it was, it sold like wildfire. Crowds flocked to disc jockey Alan Freed's rock 'n' roll tours, where 10 bands performed in one night. Chuck Berry, Jerry Lee Lewis, Buddy Holly, Bill Haley, Carl Perkins, Little Richard, Eddie Cochran, the Coasters, Fats Domino, and the Everly Brothers became teen heroes, recording

Elvis thrills an enraptured audience during the shooting of his 1957 movie *Loving You*. The film's story paralleled his own sudden rise to fame and gave him a chance to demonstrate his startling moves in several stunning performance scenes.

chart-topping radio hits that are still played around the world every day.

At the pinnacle stood Elvis Presley, who somehow actually accelerated his breakneck pace in 1957. On top of performing in a hit movie, 10 TV performances, and 100 sold-out concerts in 1956, he had sold nearly 3 million albums, along with 7 times that many Elvis products, such as photos, watches, handbags, combs, and dolls. Manager Tom Parker saw no reason for the king of rock 'n' roll to slow down.

In 1957, Presley starred in two movies, *Loving You,* in which he received his first on-screen kiss, from costar Jana Lund, and *Jailhouse Rock,* which is generally recognized as the best film he ever made. *Loving You* is a romanticized retelling of Presley's rise to fame, but the concert footage—with raving teenaged girls and the band's exciting music—accurately conveys the excitement of an Elvis Presley performance. Presley had brought his parents out to Hollywood while the film was being made, and they even appeared in a crowd scene at the end.

Jailhouse Rock is a gritty black-and-white movie in which Presley played rebellious prison inmate Vince Everett. Falsely accused of manslaughter, Everett takes up singing in prison and skyrockets to fame after his release. Presley choreographed the now legendary dance sequence accompanying the film's title song, which describes a rocking party in the county jail. That song, along with a pair of tunes from Presley's third RCA album, "All Shook Up" and "Teddy Bear," topped the pop charts.

In their spare time, the band continued to tour, driving overnight to one-show engagements all over the Northeast and into Canada, playing at football stadiums and using a flatbed truck as a stage. Though the loudspeakers in use at the time could not carry their music very far, they drew large audiences. The quartet of Presley, Scotty Moore, Bill Black, and D. J. Fontana had become the most exciting rock 'n' roll band in the world, pushing each other to new heights with every performance. Colonel Tom Parker shrewdly refused to let his star join the rock 'n' roll tours that packaged several performers together in one concert. Fans who came to see Elvis saw only Elvis, reinforcing the notion that he stood on a different plane from the other rock 'n' rollers.

When Elvis's parents returned to Memphis from Hollywood they helped their son select a new home, eventually settling on a large, stately house on 13 acres of farmland in Whitehaven, a nearby suburb. The 18-room, columned mansion had been built in 1939 of pink field-

Elvis Presley plays lord of the manor in front of Graceland, the mansion on 13 acres of farmland that he bought in 1957.

stone and named Graceland. Presley spent $500,000 to renovate the estate, adding five rooms, an eight-foot high stone fence, and the now famous wrought iron "music gate," which shows two guitar players and a string of musical notes, supposedly the opening bars to Presley's tune "Love Me Tender." Though Elvis Presley had moved from house to house nearly every year of his young life, he would never have to move again. Graceland would be his home for the rest of his life.

As Elvis became wealthier and more famous, however, his bandmates did not share in his glory. Bill Black and Scotty Moore, who had been there from the beginning, rehearsing with Presley when he was still an unknown truck driver from Memphis, were still being paid a flat $200 a week by the parsimonious Colonel Parker. From

Elvis reassures his concerned parents, who learned five days before Christmas in 1957 that their son had been drafted into the armed forces.

that money they had to shell out their own touring expenses. Black and Moore had played a huge part in creating the rock 'n' roll sound. Young guitarists and bass players to this day copy them note for note. But after wrapping up a grueling concert tour in the fall of 1957, both musicians called it quits. This unfortunate move broke up one of the most important and innovative bands in American music.

Still reeling from their departure, Presley recorded an album of Christmas songs. One tune from this session, "Blue Christmas," has become a holiday standard. But at the time, many radio stations refused to play Presley's Christmas music, claiming that the hip-shaking rock 'n' roller had besmirched the religious holiday. Presley was clearly hurt by the attacks on his character, but the millions of fans who bought his album buoyed his spirits. At Graceland he decorated a white Christmas tree with red ornaments, laid down a snowy white rug, and enjoyed his most storybook Christmas yet with his parents. Singing at the piano, none of them dreamed that this would be their last Christmas together.

Five days before Christmas the U.S. Army sent Elvis a present he had been expecting for some time—his induction notice. The piece of paper demanded that he begin basic training in one month. Colonel Tom Parker pulled strings to postpone Presley's induction for a few more weeks so he could complete filming his fourth movie, *King Creole,* but there was never any question that the king of rock 'n' roll would accept the call to military service.

When the news got out, reporters hurried to Graceland for photos of Presley holding his draft notice in front of the Christmas tree. Afterward, he and his friends drove all over Memphis buying up all the fireworks they could find. Then they went into the pasture and played a game Presley called "War" until 3:00 A.M. The game involved lighting the fireworks and throwing them at each other. Amazingly, no one was hurt. In this extremely dangerous way Presley let off steam built up from his astonishing three-year rise to fame and fortune, and its sudden interruption. He must have known that joining the army would put all his dreams on hold. But as he dodged blazing bottle rockets and cherry bombs in the chilly pasture, whooping and screaming with his pals, no one could say whether his skyrocketing career was on the way up or down.

6 · G.I. Blues

OCK STAR JOHN LENNON, always one of Elvis Presley's most astute fans, said two remarkable things about his hero. Thinking of all the youngsters like himself whose lives were changed by rock 'n' roll, he declared, "Before there was Elvis, there was nothing." Years later, when a reporter asked him to comment on Presley's death, Lennon replied with absolute seriousness, "Elvis died when he went into the army."

When Presley joined the military, millions of his teenaged fans felt his loss just as profoundly. Newspapers across the nation showed photographs of the rock 'n' roll star sitting in an army barber's chair, having his glossy pompadour shaved. Stuffy grown-ups gloated about the king of rock 'n' roll trading in his blue suede shoes for army boots. How could a man whose music seemed to be all about rebellion and freedom and fun give up his spontaneous dance moves for a soldier's grim lockstep?

Apparently, Presley never gave the move a second thought. In his opinion, just because he was a millionaire singer and movie star did not mean he deserved special treatment. Though many Elvis fans felt betrayed by their

Elvis submits to the shears of a military barber upon his induction into the U.S. Army on March 25, 1958.

idol, others saw in his army induction a noble humility. As one fan said approvingly, "Elvis never forgot where he came from. He knew he was 'just folks' like everybody else." This notion of Elvis Presley as a heroic everyman would only grow among fans in the years to come.

Before Presley joined the army, however, he had many loose ends to tie up. He spent the early part of 1958 filming his fourth movie, *King Creole,* in New Orleans. Like *Loving You* and *Jailhouse Rock,* this musical drama had Elvis playing a young unknown singer on his way to

Elvis dons his new army uniform and prepares for boot camp. Although he could probably have met the legal requirements of military service by perform-ing for the troops, Elvis instead became a private in the army and was sent to Germany, where his experi-ence as a truck driver won him an assignment driving a jeep.

fame and glory. In *King Creole* his character's musical talents are discovered while he scrubs floors in a French Quarter nightclub.

Presley must have given one of his trademark smirks to recall the many Memphis nightclub floors he had swept as a teenager just for a chance to sing onstage for a moment. After completing the day's filming, though, Presley had to stay locked in his hotel room, protected from the thousands of fans who prowled the streets searching for their idol.

King Creole was an old-fashioned Hollywood movie, full of gangsters and guns. When the movie opened over the summer, Elvis received good reviews for the first time. A *New York Times* critic flatly stated, "The boy can act."

With the movie finished, on March 24, 1958, Presley reported for army service at Fort Chaffee, Arkansas. He transferred a few days later to Fort Hood, Texas, for basic training. RCA records executives were dismayed at losing the singer whose records accounted for 25 percent of their sales. During a weekend pass in June, they brought Presley to Nashville to record five songs, including "A Big Hunk of Love," which reached number one on the pop music charts. RCA also issued a soundtrack album of *King Creole* when the film opened over the summer. But Elvis still had 18 months to serve in the army, and it would not be easy to keep his fans supplied with music while he was away.

Colonel Tom Parker thought he could get a better contract for his star if he made the executives wait. He told them to repackage Elvis's early hits and even talked them into issuing a press conference interview as an album. RCA's executives were stunned when each of these meager offerings sold millions of copies. Maybe the Colonel was right after all, they thought. Elvis fans *would* buy anything with their idol's picture on the cover. For the rest of Presley's career RCA issued one spotty album after another, usually including a hit song and a batch of lousy ones. Even the worst of these sold well.

During his last few weeks in Texas before being shipped overseas, Elvis moved his parents into a small house near the army base. Ever since his sudden rise to stardom, he had spent little time with his parents. Gladys had not taken the separation from her son well. Her cousin Annie Presley remembered, "after they moved to Graceland she was always saying how much she wished she was back here and poor again. 'They won't let me see Elvis,' she would say. 'They're always keeping him working somewhere or other,' or 'They're just tearing my boy's clothes off and we don't know if he's going to come back alive.'" Having made Elvis the center of her life, she found it difficult to share him with so many others. Many accounts say that in his absence she turned increasingly to alcohol, which began to destroy her health.

Elvis was shocked to see his beloved mother looking so bloated and tired when she arrived in Texas. Gladys had come down with a debilitating strain of hepatitis. She spent most of the day resting in her bedroom away from the sweltering heat and finally had to take a train back to Memphis for treatment by her doctor. One week later, that doctor called Elvis and told him to come back to Graceland in a hurry.

Elvis and his father stayed at Gladys's side in the hospital for several days. When she died, on August 14, 1958, the two men whom she had cared for and supported for so long cried inconsolably. One newspaper interview described Elvis saying that "her death 'broke my heart.'" The account continued, "Tears streamed down his cheeks. He cried throughout the interview. 'She's all we lived for,' he sobbed. 'She was always my best girl.'" Papers across the country printed photographs of Vernon and Elvis sobbing with their arms around each other.

Mrs. Presley's favorite gospel group, the Blackwoods, sang at her funeral. At the cemetery, reporters heard her son cry out, "Goodbye darling, goodbye. I love you so much. You know how much. I lived my whole life for you! Oh, God! Everything I have is gone." Bodyguards eventually had to pry the singer's hands from the coffin in order to lower it into the ground. Devastated, Elvis spent the next nine days alone in his bedroom. All his life he had wanted to pay his mother back for her sacrifices, to make her old age a time of leisure. But now she had died at the age of 46. Her son would never get over losing her. As his aunt Lillian Smith said, "After Gladys died, he changed completely. He didn't seem like Elvis ever again."

Vernon and Elvis Presley mourn the death of Elvis's mother, Gladys. At her burial the distraught singer cried out, "I lived my whole life for you! Oh, God! Everything I have is gone."

Six weeks later, still heartbroken, Private Presley traveled with the Third Armored Division to the quaint, cobblestoned town of Bad Nauheim, West Germany. He spent the next year and a half there with his father and his grandmother, Minnie Mae Presley, in a rented house near the army base. Minnie Mae cooked up rashers of bacon with mustard for Elvis's favorite sandwiches, and Vernon organized a nightly autograph hour for the crowds of German fräuleins who gathered near the army base in hopes of seeing their idol. Elvis, the former truck driver, was assigned to drive a jeep. In his off-hours he began to study karate, which would become a lifelong passion.

It was impossible to pretend, however, that Elvis was just another soldier. The king of rock 'n' roll was just as well known in Germany as he was in the United States. In every beer hall in the country his music ruled the jukeboxes. Wherever he went girls surrounded him. But after three years of an unbelievably grueling rise to stardom, his time in the army provided something of a break. Thousands of miles away from his Memphis cronies, with no one begging him to make a movie or a record, he tried to make sense of his fame, living the workaday life he had miraculously escaped and would never know again.

It was at this time that Presley met an amazingly precocious 14-year-old girl, Priscilla Beaulieu, the stepdaughter of an army officer. When Elvis saw her for the first time, he exclaimed, "She looks like an angel!" Thinking the beautiful girl was in her late teens, he began to chat with her. When he discovered that she was in just the ninth grade, he said, "Why, you're just a baby."

"Thanks," Priscilla replied curtly.

Caught off guard, the rock 'n' roll star responded, "Well. Seems the little girl has spunk."

Presley spent the evening playing the piano and singing all of his hit songs to the young girl. He then asked if

Sixteen-year-old Priscilla Beaulieu waves good-bye to Elvis Presley on March 3, 1960, as he boards a plane to return to the United States at the end of his two-year term of military service in Germany. Elvis met and began dating Priscilla when she was 14 years old and in the ninth grade.

he could see her the next night, and the next. Priscilla felt as if she were Cinderella being chosen by a handsome prince. But Elvis always behaved politely, promising never to harm her in any way. Late into the night they would sit holding hands in his room while she listened to his stories about his beloved mother. As Elvis told her, "I really like you, Priscilla. You're refreshing. It's nice to talk to someone from back home. I miss that. It gets a little lonely here."

On March 2, 1960, Elvis Presley wrapped up his tour of duty and flew back to the United States with his army buddies. He left Priscilla his combat jacket and the sergeant's stripes he had recently earned, made her promise to write, and then waved to her from the top of the airplane ramp. She rode home in tears with her parents, convinced that her amazing storybook romance was over.

Meanwhile, back in New York, Colonel Tom Parker had put together a grand welcome home ceremony for

Although he had not performed in two years, Elvis's return to the United States in 1960 was greeted with wild enthusiasm, and his career picked up right where it had left off.

his only client. He rented a railroad magnate's private railway car for the long ride back to Memphis, and at every station along the way crowds gathered to cheer. Already the nation's record stores had placed a million orders for Elvis's new album, which had not even been recorded yet. Frank Sinatra was offering Elvis the un-heard-of sum of $125,000 to sing two songs on his upcoming TV special. In Hollywood, movie executives wanted their biggest box office star to begin filming a new movie as soon as possible. If Elvis had entertained any doubts about his lasting fame during his tour of duty, he forgot them now.

After two years in the army the king of rock 'n' roll was eager to get back to work. Before the month was out he drove to Nashville to begin recording a new album. Elvis convinced drummer D. J. Fontana and guitarist Scotty Moore to record with him again, but his old friend, bassist Bill Black, refused to rejoin the band. He was still angry over being paid so poorly in the past. RCA hired pianist Floyd Cramer and the gospel quartet the Jordanaires to help out. With guitarist Chet Atkins pro-ducing, Elvis recorded an extraordinary set of songs in just one month.

Elvis's bandmates were amazed to hear that the singer's voice had actually improved in the army. He had always displayed a wide vocal range, but now for the first time he could downshift smoothly from a keening high tenor to a deep and soothing baritone. In songs like "Stuck on You," "It's Now or Never," and "Fame and Fortune," Presley gave some of the most masterful per-formances of his career. Every song released from this session became an overnight million-seller. And the jewel of the bunch—"Are You Lonesome Tonight?"—quickly became his signature song.

Though some of the songs Elvis recorded at this time—among them "Such a Night" and "Reconsider

Baby"—were as rocking as anything he had ever sung, most of his new work could not be called rock 'n' roll. Following the advice of his manager Colonel Tom Parker, Elvis determined now to make a name for himself

as a romantic crooner in the tradition of his heroes Dean Martin, Billy Eckstine, and Frank Sinatra. Parker apparently believed that rock 'n' roll music was just a passing fad, and he wanted to make sure that Elvis's success would last.

The romantic ballads Presley recorded now clearly fit the crooner image. To complete his transformation, when Elvis appeared on Sinatra's TV special in May 1960, he cheerfully donned a tuxedo and sang a duet with the old master. No longer the wild-haired rebel, Presley was becoming a quintessential pop singer. If he lost fans among the young men who had idolized his reckless image, he gained them among women. Elvis's silken voice could still make them swoon.

Always an avid lover of gospel music, Elvis recorded
his first gospel album in Nashville, *His Hand in Mine.*
The album was a lovingly inspired collection of spirituals
and hymns Presley had been singing in church since

Elvis records with the popular
gospel group the Jordanaires,
who were his backup singers
from 1956 to 1967.

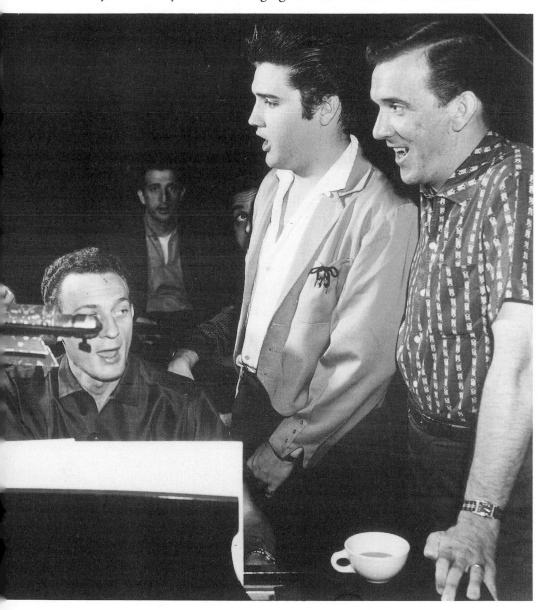

childhood. On "Peace in the Valley" and "Swing Low Sweet Chariot," the singer harmonized beautifully with his customary backup group, the Jordanaires, performing in the quartet style he had learned from the all-night gospel sings he had attended as a teenager.

In May, Elvis traveled back to Hollywood to make his fifth movie. Having received good reviews for his final prearmy performance in *King Creole,* he hoped to begin building a career as a serious actor. But when he looked at the script for *G.I. Blues,* he realized he was being offered just more of the same pablum he had been filming before. The movie producers thought they knew what fans liked most in an Elvis Presley movie—a thinly disguised slice of the singer's life (in this case his years in the army), some songs, and a happy ending. *G.I. Blues* hardly even called on Presley to act.

Furious with the lousy script, Elvis called Germany long-distance to complain to Priscilla Beaulieu, "I just finished looping the picture, and I hate it. I feel like an idiot breaking into a song while I'm talking to some chick on a train." She could not understand how the most famous actor in Hollywood could be roped into making a movie he hated. Reluctant to admit that he was unwilling to challenge the authority of Colonel Parker, with whom he had become as obedient as he was toward his parents, he glumly replied, "Already been paid. They all seem to think it's wonderful. I'm miserable."

Elvis's fans seemed to think the movie was wonderful, too. *G.I. Blues* became the 14th highest-grossing movie of the year, and the soundtrack album stayed at number one on the pop charts longer than any of his previous albums. As Colonel Parker had said, Elvis's fans would buy anything with his name on it. When Elvis complained, the Colonel just grinned and said, "How do you argue with this kind of success? It's like telling Maxwell House to change their coffee formula when the stuff is selling like no tomorrow." Presley could only shrug and hope for a better script next time.

On March 25, 1961, Presley performed live in Honolulu, Hawaii, at a benefit in honor of the U.S.S. *Arizona,* the battleship that had been sunk by Japanese bombs in Pearl Harbor on December 7, 1941. No one knew it at the time, but it would be the end of the decade before the king of rock 'n' roll gave another live show. For better or worse, Presley had set his sights on a Hollywood career. Any fan who wanted to see Elvis in the 1960s would have to buy a ticket to the movies.

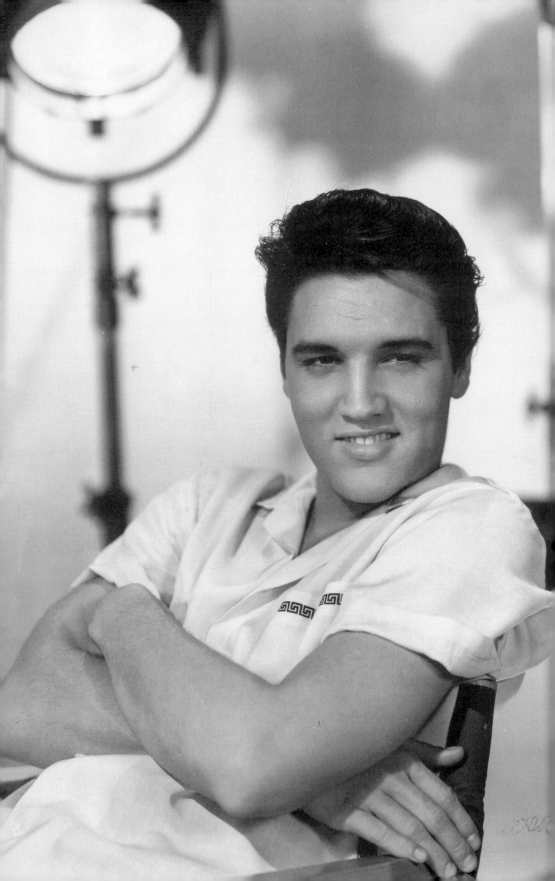

7 Cryin' in the Chapel

FROM 1961 TO 1968, ELVIS PRESLEY starred in 28 movies. Some are good, some are just all right, and some are plain awful. As critic Stanley Booth wrote, all of these star vehicles have two things in common: "None lost money, none is contingent at any point upon reality."

After the musical comedy *G.I. Blues,* Presley demanded the opportunity to make a serious film. In *Flaming Star,* released during the Christmas holidays in 1960, he had his chance. Director Don Siegel (who later won fame for the film *Dirty Harry,* starring Clint Eastwood) organized a cast of notable actors to tell a tale of racial prejudice set in the Old West. Presley played the leading role of Pacer Burton, the half-breed son of a white settler and a Kiowa Indian. Amid an Indian uprising, Burton is forced to choose sides between his Indian family and his white one.

Though Elvis held his own as an actor in this movie, his fans seemed disappointed at not seeing him sing on-screen. *Flaming Star* performed poorly at the box office. In *Wild in the Country,* his next film, Elvis took another shot at a serious acting role and again seemed to let his fans down. Presley

---

The Elvis Presley of the 1960s was a far cry from the rock 'n' roll rebel of the 1950s. He withdrew from live performing and made more than two dozen movies that relied on his good looks and mild-mannered charm. Though he sang in almost every movie, his music in this period broke little new ground.

This publicity shot for *Blue Hawaii* characterized the new Elvis, as envisioned by Colonel Parker. Most of his movies in the 1960s could be described as light, formulaic fluff.

played an arrogant southern hothead who is eventually saved from his violent streak by three women, played by Millie Perkins, Hope Lange, and newcomer Tuesday Weld.

Learning from their mistake with *Flaming Star,* the movie's producers attempted to attract audiences by adding four songs to the script. It did not work. *Teen* magazine's readers voted Presley and Weld their Damp Raincoat Award as the year's most disappointing on-screen romance. The movie barely broke even at the box office. Consequently, Elvis succumbed to Colonel Parker's suggestions, agreeing to go back to the musical comedies he hated so much.

Blue Hawaii, his next project, is the blueprint for all the movies that followed. It is far and away the most popular film Presley ever made. Filmed at spectacular Waikiki Beach, *Blue Hawaii* centers on a young man's indecision over whether to join his father's pineapple business or play music with his friends on the beach. It is chock-full of songs—14 in all—and includes one of

Elvis's most successful singles, "Can't Help Falling in Love with You."

Blue Hawaii opened on Thanksgiving Day, 1961, and grossed $5 million by New Year's Day. The soundtrack album became his biggest seller ever. That was the end of Elvis's career as a serious movie actor. If once he had been touted as the successor to firebrands such as James Dean and Marlon Brando, from now on he would be saddled with more of the same bland projects. They all involved beautiful travelogue settings, skimpily clad young women, a bunch of songs, and very little in the way of plot. Elvis's fans wanted to see him in silly musical comedies, and they got their wish.

The titles of these movies alone give a sense of their frivolity: *Viva Las Vegas*; *Paradise, Hawaiian Style*; *Fun in Acapulco*; and *Girls! Girls! Girls!* are typical examples. Whether Elvis played a race-car driver, a ski instructor, a circus performer, or a rodeo rider, the scripts were pretty much the same: boy meets girl, boy pursues girl, boy gets

Actor Jeremy Slate takes a punch from Elvis Presley in the 1962 film *Girls! Girls! Girls!*

girl. In each movie he starred opposite a different Hollywood starlet, among them Ursula Andress, Ann-Margret, Juliet Prowse, and Joan Blackman. Colonel Parker made sure Elvis always played a morally up-right straight-shooter. He rejected many interesting roles that asked his client to appear as less than perfect. Whatever else happened, Elvis sang an average of nine songs per movie.

Elvis's directors learned to knock out a movie in record time. The worst of the batch—*Kissin' Cousins* (1963)—took

just 17 days to film. Some years saw the appearance of as many as four Elvis movies. Drive-in theaters ran double bills of his latest projects. The movies made the ideal background for teenage couples hugging and kissing in their cars: the music was fun, the scenery was romantic, and the plots were easy to summarize the next day for stern parents who wondered whether one had watched the movie or not.

Elvis was not making art, but he was making buckets of money. By 1965, 17 of his films had achieved a gross of between 125 million and 135 million dollars. The highest paid actor in Hollywood, Presley was guaranteed $1 million and half the profits from each movie.

RCA released a soundtrack album for each film. Guitarist Scotty Moore recalls that Elvis balked at recording these albums because he knew how lousy most of the songs were: "We'd go to the studio at around four or five in the afternoon and Elvis'd show up at eight or nine. He wouldn't hit a lick or a note till three, four in the morning. He'd already heard the material and he was just dreading it. He knew they were bad songs. He hated all of it, just about."

In the old days, Presley had driven his band to record up to 60 takes of a song until they got it exactly right. Now he just concentrated on one or two songs that he liked and coasted through the rest. Some of the soundtrack songs are considered to be awful (the worst may be a ditty called

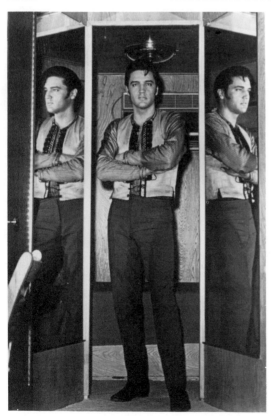

Elvis, dressed in a costume from one of his movies, poses before a three-way mirror.

"Do the Clam"), but "Viva Las Vegas," "Little Sister," "King of the Whole Wide World," and "Cryin' in the Chapel" succeed in transcending their sappy medium.

The irony of Elvis's work in the 1960s is that although he raked in millions and millions of dollars, he was reduced to a laughingstock in the process. As an actor, he seemed like a handsome but lightweight clown. As a singer, he seemed like a pale cartoon of his former rocking self. Strapped to contracts for bad movies and records, surrounded by bodyguards and pals who were paid to laugh at every lame joke he made, and swarmed by beautiful women, Presley gradually slipped into a strange, unreal existence, and his life began to look eerily like his movies.

No matter how much money he spent—at one point he owned 50 expensive cars and a private jet—there was always more coming in. Presley donated money to charities, gave Cadillacs away to waitresses in restaurants, and bedecked friends with bulky golden jewelry. He threw lavish parties every night in Hollywood, wrecking the furniture by playing wild football games in the living room or frightening his guests—most of them young women—with displays of his karate prowess.

Memphis became a private playground, where he lived out fantasies he could not have dreamed of as a poverty-stricken teenager. The fans who stood at the gates of Graceland kept Presley locked in the house during the day, but he frequently rented a neighborhood movie theater or skating rink after-hours or threw all-night parties at local amusement parks, riding the bumper cars and roller coaster until dawn.

Two years after leaving West Germany, Presley had Priscilla Beaulieu and her parents flown to Los Angeles for a visit. After touring Hollywood and spending Christmas with the Presleys at Graceland, the Beaulieus agreed to let their 16-year-old daughter stay in Memphis with her famous boyfriend, with the firm stipulation that Elvis saw to it that Priscilla graduated from high school.

Elvis knew that the morally correct image he projected on the movie screen jarred with his affection for a teenager, so he made sure to keep his relationship with Priscilla a secret. While he filmed movies at the country's glamour spots, she lived at Graceland with Elvis's grandmother, Minnie Mae Presley, and attended an all-girls high school, Immaculate Conception. When Elvis came back to town between movies, he lavished fancy clothes and jewelry upon her. Soon he convinced her to dye her hair jet black like his and began to call her Sattnin, a nickname he had previously used only with his beloved mother. At night she joined him at the movie theater or amusement park, finding it humorous that he behaved more like a teenager than she did.

Elvis coasted along in this way until 1965, when his record sales began to slip. That year a new wave of popular music known as the British Invasion took over radio playlists. Young English bands, such as the Beatles, the Rolling Stones, and the Dave Clark Five, made Elvis Presley—at the age of 28—seem like a washed-up old man. Most of these bands revered the early rock 'n' roll stars who had inspired them. The Beatles even visited Elvis at Graceland, sitting nervously on his sofa until he loosened them up by saying, "If y'all aren't gonna say anything, I'm going to bed." With Elvis at the piano, they sang old rhythm-and-blues songs together until 2:00 A.M.

Most of Elvis's fans had grown up by this time, and many now had children who raved about the Beatles' appearance on "The Ed Sullivan Show" much as they themselves had cheered for Elvis. Those children spent their allowances on records by the British bands. With that the rock 'n' roll era ended and the rock music era began. In 1965, Elvis charted only one top-10 single, "Cryin' in the Chapel." His soundtrack albums slipped

Elvis, a major Hollywood star, reaches out of a car window to sign a snapshot.

lower on the top-10 list. In 1966, as Beatlemania swept the country, only one of his singles, "Love Letters," reached the top 20. The next year none did.

As the tumultuous 1960s drew to a close, Elvis continued to fulfill his movie contracts, though each film earned less money than the one before. Playing the part of a country squire, he bought horses and riding lessons for himself, Priscilla, and his many bodyguards. Though the Vietnam War was dividing the country and rock music ruled the pop charts, Elvis seemed oblivious to all the upheaval, living in the protective bubble that Graceland had become.

In 1967, Elvis bought a ranch, which he named the Circle G for Graceland, and moved his 18 horses into the barn. He installed mobile homes for his friends and gave each of them a brand new truck. Even the plumber and the painter received a truck. His father pleaded with him to stop pouring money into the ranch, but Elvis was delighted with his new hobby. The spending spree continued until, at Vernon's urging, Colonel Parker came up with yet another movie project, *Clambake,* forcing Elvis to depart for Hollywood. Elvis became so depressed that he put on 30 pounds, which then had to be burned off with the aid of amphetamines.

Perhaps Elvis's greatest achievement during the mid-1960s was his 1967 gospel album *How Great Thou Art.* In making this record, he went back to his old perfectionist ways, working all day on a song until it was just right. He hired his gospel idol Jake Hess, formerly of the Statesmen Quartet, along with his new quartet, the Imperials, and brought in a female quartet to give the music the fulsome sound of a mixed choir. A choice group of Nashville session musicians made up the band. On the album cover, Elvis posed in a Sunday suit in front of a church steeple. *How Great Thou Art* sold a million copies and won the only Grammy award Elvis ever received.

Meanwhile, in Memphis, Priscilla Beaulieu had graduated from high school and come of age. At last the couple's secret love could be revealed to the public. On May 1, 1967, after living together for five years, Elvis and Priscilla were married.

The arrangements for the wedding were handled by Colonel Parker, and much as he did with Elvis's career, the Colonel took complete control. In order to keep a step ahead of the press, on the day before the wedding he had Elvis and Priscilla drive from Los Angeles to Palm Springs in order to give the impression that the ceremony would be held there. Instead, before the sun came up on their wedding day, they caught a plane to Las Vegas, where they had an appointment at 7:00 A.M. to get their marriage license at the city clerk's office. From there they rushed to the Aladdin Hotel for a hurried ceremony. Without telling Elvis, the Colonel had told several of

On May 1, 1967, Elvis Presley and Priscilla Beaulieu were married by Nevada Supreme Court justice David Zenoff (left) in Las Vegas. At right is Priscilla's sister and maid of honor, Michelle Beaulieu. The exhausted couple had driven from Los Angeles to Palm Springs the previous day, then stayed up all night to fly to Las Vegas as part of a plan by Colonel Parker to dodge the press.

Elvis's closest friends that they could not attend the wedding because there was no room. By the time Elvis found out, it was too late.

Nobody but the Colonel was too pleased with the proceedings. Elvis's old friend Red West, for one, was so angry that he refused even to attend the reception. As for Priscilla, she wrote years later in *Elvis and Me* (1985):

> I sometimes look back at all the commotion of that week and wonder how things could have gotten so out of hand. I wish I'd had the strength then to say, 'Wait a minute, this is *our* wedding, fans or no fans, press or no press. Let us invite whomever we want, and have it wherever we want!'

But the elaborate preparations that had so inconvenienced family, friends—and the bride and groom—still did not provide the couple with an opportunity to savor the occasion in privacy. Priscilla commented sadly, "I would have given anything for one moment alone with my husband. But we were immediately rushed out for a photo session, then a nationwide press conference, and finally a reception, with more photographers." The couple spent their wedding night in Palm Springs, returning to the seclusion of Graceland the following day.

On February 1, 1968, exactly nine months after the wedding, Priscilla gave birth to a daughter, whom they named Lisa Marie. Cornered by a reporter at the hospital, the new father said, "I'm a happy, but shaky man." Although they were delighted to have a healthy baby, once again their plans to finally spend some time alone or travel together would have to be postponed.

Elvis and Priscilla Presley proudly display their four-day-old baby, Lisa Marie, who was born on February 1, 1968.

In 1968, musical producer Steve Binder asked Elvis to appear in a televised Christmas special. The singer had not performed on TV in several years, and he did not see any reason to now. But Binder, a fan of Elvis's early rock 'n' roll records, came up with a scheme to show Elvis how important such a move would be. Binder realized that Presley was insulated from the real world—reportedly he did not even know what a can of soda pop cost—and had lost touch with his fans. He dared Elvis to take a walk down Sunset Boulevard in Los Angeles, just to see if anybody would notice him.

At first Presley laughed at the suggestion. If he ventured beyond the confines of his private rooms he would be mobbed with fans, he argued. Binder replied, "Wanna bet?" Beginning to grow curious, Presley agreed to the dare. The next day Elvis, Binder, and a couple of bodyguards stepped out of a Cadillac onto the Sunset Strip and spent the next hour strolling amid the colorful hippie crowd. Not a single person recognized him. Growing frustrated, Presley began to hum a few bars of a song. People pushed past him without a word. Even when he began to shake his hips and sing, no one paid attention. Finally he grunted, "C'mon boys," and climbed back into the Cadillac feeling like a forgotten man.

The longtime king of rock 'n' roll had suffered a rude awakening. He asked Binder what plans he had for the TV special. Binder—the director of the musical TV show "Hullabaloo"—wanted to give the king of rock 'n' roll a chance to reclaim his crown by performing all the greatest songs of his career. He promised that he would spare no expense to make the TV special work. Despite his bruised feelings, Elvis rose to the challenge. "Let's do it," he snarled.

8 ★ I Was the One

AS A JUNIOR-HIGH-SCHOOL STUDENT in Tupelo, Mississippi, Elvis Presley had won over his classmates with music. At stuffy Humes High School in Memphis he had done the same thing. Having changed the world by introducing its teenagers to the liberating cry of rock 'n' roll, he now had to make one more effort to prove himself. In the face of a whole new generation of rock stars, after years of making silly movies, Elvis at the age of 33 was right back where he had started, a laughingstock at the back of the class. Once again he would have to rely on his music to earn people's respect.

In order to perform rock 'n' roll on television again, Elvis Presley had to fight Colonel Parker every step of the way. The Colonel told NBC executives, "He's gonna do 24 Christmas songs and say, 'Merry Christmas, everybody.'" But Steve Binder had a different idea. "Nobody has ever seen him in a TV setting where he was able to talk about his life, as a dancer, performer, the concert ability—we should be doing that!" he said.

In the end, Elvis went along with Binder's plan, even though he admitted that trying to reclaim his crown in an era of flamboyant stars like James

---

Elvis Presley burst back onto the rock 'n' roll scene with this December 3, 1968, television special—one of his few performances not controlled by Colonel Parker. Parker had insisted, "He's gonna do 24 Christmas songs and say, 'Merry Christmas, everybody.'" Instead, Elvis wore black leather and dusted off his greatest rock 'n' roll hits, regaining much of the credibility he had lost in the 1960s.

Brown, Mick Jagger, and Jim Morrison made him feel "sheer terror." While Binder organized the show, Elvis flew to Hawaii to work himself into shape. He returned tanned and slim, looking as good as he ever had. Author Dave Marsh wrote, "Elvis Presley was a singularly handsome man for most of his years but on the comeback special he was radiant, a great American beauty, the idealized Everyman come to life."

The TV Christmas special opened with a red neon logo spelling "ELVIS" across the screen and Elvis's voice singing these opening lines: "Lookin' for trouble? You came to the right place!" Suddenly he appeared, dressed in a tight-fitting black leather jacket and slacks and flailing at a red electric guitar. Surrounded by guitar-playing dancers, Elvis seemed irrepressible, putting all he had learned about music and performing into every line. As Greil Marcus wrote, "It was the finest music of his life. If ever there was music that bleeds, this was it. Nothing came easy that night, and he gave everything he had—more than anyone knew was there."

Elvis performed half of the show on a round stage no bigger than a boxing ring. Then he sat onstage with guitarist Scotty Moore and drummer D. J. Fontana, from his original band, and a few other musicians. At this point Elvis had the opportunity to chat with his audience and to reminisce about his long career. He still looked pained to remember how comedian Steve Allen had made him sing to a basset hound. He joked about the Jacksonville performance where just the wiggle of his pinky finger had caused a riot. But the effort of putting his 14-year career into perspective seemed to overwhelm him. Again and again, he returned to the music, performing even such early hits as "That's All Right (Mama)" and "One Night." His voice soared with unbridled passion, but with a new maturity that made the old songs seem fresh again, and even more volatile than before. In one hour on national

Elvis announces his return to live performing at a press conference in 1969.

television in 1968, the king of rock 'n' roll reclaimed his crown.

Backstage afterward, as his bodyguards used razors to cut the sweat-soaked leather slacks off his legs, Elvis exclaimed, "I want to go out and perform again!" Right after Christmas he challenged Memphis recording engineer Chips Moman to help him make a great record. Moman knew how to use all the modern studio technology that Elvis had never bothered with before. His tiny American Studios had charted a string of 22 hits in the past three years. With just four days' notice, he pulled together session musicians and backup singers, rehearsed two dozen songs, and waited nervously for Elvis's arrival.

Elvis pushed Moman and his band through a series of grueling all-night recording sessions in January 1969. Everyone took a break, then recorded six more marathon sessions in February. The result was some of the greatest music of Presley's career, a rousing mix of pop and soul music that sounded more contemporary than anything the singer had recorded in years. Once again, Elvis had reclaimed all the types of music that he really loved—gospel, country, blues, and sentimental ballads—combining them to make a whole new sound. Rock critic Peter Guralnick, admitting that Elvis had been a joke for years, wrote, "I think this music is flatly and unequivocally the equal of anything he has ever done." The first single, "In the Ghetto," became his first top-10 hit since 1965. The second release, "Suspicious Minds," went to number one. In all, five top-20 singles and two gold albums came out of the sessions.

With a batch of new hits to sing, Elvis geared up to tour for the first time in a decade. But first he had some unfinished business to take care of in Hollywood. Colonel Parker reminded him that he still had to make three more movies to fulfill his latest contract. At first Elvis flatly refused, but he finally agreed on the condition that he get another chance to play a serious acting role.

At his insistence, Elvis's last three movies broke away from his usual musical comedy formula. In the low-budget western *Charro,* Elvis played a rough-looking former outlaw standing up to the members of his old posse. The advertising posters proclaimed, "a different kind of role . . . a different kind of man." For the first time in years, Elvis did not have to sing on-screen. Unfortunately, his fans were unimpressed.

In *The Trouble with Girls,* Elvis played the ringleader of a carnival show. He did not appear on-screen until the movie was a third of the way over, however, because most of the action was given over to the carnival troupe.

Reviewers wrote that Elvis looked more handsome than ever but still had a long way to go to become a serious actor.

The last movie Elvis made was the melodramatic *A Change of Habit,* costarring television actress Mary Tyler Moore. Elvis played a doctor in an inner-city clinic, Moore a nun who swapped her habit for street clothes at work. The two fall in love, and Moore's character is forced to choose between Elvis and the church. None of these three movies provided an acting breakthrough for Elvis, but they allowed him to end his acting career honorably. Whatever else can be said about Presley's movies, as Colonel Parker often reminded him, none of his 33 films lost money at the box office.

In July 1969, Elvis triumphantly returned to the stage with a $1 million contract for a two-week run at the International Hotel in Las Vegas. For the bulk of the 1970s he would be known primarily as a Las Vegas performer, typically performing more than 100 shows per year.

Elvis's return to live performing provided an escape from the endless string of lightweight movies he had been making, but his career soon leveled off again into an exhausting and repetitive series of performances in Las Vegas.

Elvis finally achieved his dream of performing live again on July 31, 1969. For a month he had rehearsed with a red-hot new band that included Southern blues guitarist James Burton, drummer Ronnie Tutt, bassist Jerry Scheff, and pianist Larry Muhoberac. He hired his favorite gospel quartet, the Imperials, to sing backup harmonies, along with the female quartet the Sweet Inspirations, and even brought in an orchestra to fill the stage. No longer content to be known as merely the king of rock 'n' roll, Elvis hired a leather craftsman to make a huge belt, like the ones worn by boxing champions, with a bejeweled buckle proclaiming him the "World's Greatest Entertainer."

Elvis's enormous band gave its first performance at the brand new International Hotel in Las Vegas. Colonel Parker had won a deal that promised Elvis $1 million for a two-week engagement, with two shows nightly. By starting his tour with a long run in one place, Elvis hoped to iron out the rough spots before hitting the road in earnest. Even with such a talented group of musicians backing him up, he was nervous about performing live again. He flew his first producer, Sam Phillips, in from Memphis for moral support. *New York Times* reviewer Ellen Willis observed that "Elvis was clearly unsure of himself, worried that he wouldn't get through to people after all those years, and relieved and happy when he realized we were with him."

Chatting and joking with the audience, Elvis worked through his early hits, mixing in rock 'n' roll songs with romantic ballads. He turned "Suspicious Minds" into an eight-minute orchestral extravaganza and closed with a heart-wrenching version of his ballad "Can't Help Falling in Love with You." The crowd greeted every tune with standing ovations. A recording of the concert, *Elvis in Person: At the International Hotel,* captured the excitement of this comeback performance.

Elvis did not change his performing style much in the coming years, but he drastically changed his attire. The man who had been a controversial rebel now understood that he had won all of his battles. The conqueror took to wearing fancy costumes with enormous collars and be-jeweled capes onstage. Some bore lightning bolts down the front, like the costume of his favorite childhood comic-book hero, Captain Marvel, Jr. Others were stylized karate outfits, which allowed Presley to incorporate karate moves into his dance steps. A *New York Times* reporter wrote that as one 1972 show began, "Elvis appeared, materialized, in a white suit of lights, shining with golden appliqués, the shirt front slashed to show his chest. Around his shoulders was a cape lined in a cloth of gold, its collar faced with scarlet. It was anything you wanted to call it, gaudy, vulgar, magnificent."

Elvis took his enormous band on the road right after his 35th birthday in 1970. Along with 115 shows in Las Vegas that year, the band performed one-nighters from Miami, Florida, to Portland, Oregon, at auditoriums that each held at least 10,000 people. One band member recalled, "That first tour was exciting. We felt like history was being made. When we got to a town, the people were waiting for us at the hotels and restaurants. They were at the auditorium all day, waiting."

In 1971, the city of Memphis named the street outside Graceland "Elvis Presley Boulevard." That year Elvis gave 142 shows in Las Vegas and Reno, Nevada, touring only in the month of November. The tour coincided with the release of a documentary, *Elvis: That's the Way It Is,* which told his life story as a rags-to-riches fairy tale. Colonel Parker, always determined to portray his client as an impeccably clean-cut American, personally oversaw the editing of the movie.

But if most fans believed the Colonel's portrait, Elvis's wife Priscilla knew better. Her husband had been taking amphetamines to stay awake and sleeping pills to go to sleep even while he was in the army. By the 1970s, he had added diet pills to help keep his weight down, pain killers to calm a bad back, and any number of other prescription drugs to combat various everyday complaints. When Elvis exploded in a temper tantrum, as he often did, Priscilla blamed his medications. She could only shrug wryly when her husband visited the White House in 1970 to receive a badge as an honorary federal narcotics officer from President Richard Nixon.

Many acquaintances thought Elvis was just spoiled because he could afford anything that he wanted. Before Christmas, 1970, for instance, he spent $38,000 on guns and $80,000 on cars as gifts for friends. Bored with material possessions, he had become interested in esoteric spiritual ideas. He spent hours poring over books of arcane philosophy and mysticism, and insisted that Priscilla and his friends join him in his studies. Sometimes he frightened his wife by raving for hours about "powerful forces" that were pulling stars through the galaxies. No one dared to challenge Elvis's habits. As far as most people were concerned, as long as he fulfilled his contracts and kept on singing, everything was fine.

When Elvis was not touring he stopped off in Memphis or Nashville to make records, but the country,

gospel, and Christmas tunes he recorded during the 1970s were not particularly inspired. Having won back his adoring audience, Presley grew lazy in the studio. Musician Glen D. Hardin recalled, "One Sunday night he insisted we be there by 6 o'clock and he did not show up until about Wednesday." At other times he cut studio dates short so that he could ride one of his many motorcycles.

Elvis's onstage performances began to slip, too. By his third year of touring, one reporter noted, "Elvis looked drawn, tired, and noticeably heavier than in his last Vegas appearance. He wasn't in his strongest voice." But the audiences didn't care. They squealed at the slightest flick of his cape. Middle-age women showered the stage with their underpants, inspiring one Las Vegas venue to stock fresh underwear in the ladies' rooms. Elvis did not have

One of the more bizarre moments in Elvis's life came in 1970 when he paid an impromptu call on President Richard Nixon, who granted the singer's request to be made an official drug enforcement officer. Elvis is known to have collected badges, but the true motive for his White House visit will never be known. Many say that Elvis simply wanted to help combat illegal drug use; others claim he thought the badge would allow him to safely carry illegal drugs of his own.

to try anymore. Just being there was enough to satisfy most of his audiences.

Of course, many of his fans and friends were disturbed to witness his decline. Rock journalist Lester Bangs described an encounter with one bitter fan who told him, "I got taken when I went to see Elvis Presley."

> I took my wife to see him in Vegas in '73, we paid fourteen dollars a ticket, and he came out and sang for twenty minutes. Then he fell down. Then he stood up and sang a couple more songs, then he fell down again. Finally he said, "Well . . . I might as well sing sitting as standing." So he squatted on the stage and asked the band what song they wanted to do next, but before they could answer he was complaining about the lights. "They're too bright," he says. "They hurt my eyes. Put 'em out or I don't sing a note."

Elvis and Priscilla Presley leave the courtroom arm-in-arm after their divorce on October 9, 1973, in California. The couple parted on good terms and remained friends.

So they do. So me and my wife are sitting in total blackness
listening to this guy sing songs we knew and loved . . . but
he totally *butchered* all of 'em.

Priscilla Presley eventually grew tired of her husband's
long absences, his bad temper, and his constant entourage
of bandmates and bodyguards. She had always had to put
up with an ever-present crowd of friends and relatives,
dubbed the "Memphis Mafia" by the press, that Elvis
never seemed to want to be without. Since he had settled
into his new routine of endless tours and live performances in Las Vegas, she saw him less and less. Eventually, Elvis had even refused to allow her to visit him for
his month-long stays in Vegas except for the first and last
shows of each run, and she had reason to believe that he
was filling the time by entertaining scores of young
women. Before Christmas, 1971, she left Graceland,
taking Lisa Marie with her, and moved to Los Angeles.
Though Elvis was surprised and hurt by her move, he
accepted it. On October 9, 1973, the couple officially
divorced. But they left the courthouse holding hands and
always remained friends.

Though Elvis struggled through difficult times in the
1970s, some of his performances were still magnificent.
His first concert ever at Madison Square Garden in
New York City, in June 1972, brought raves from critics.
RCA recorded all four shows to make a double album
that sold millions of copies. A charity performance in
Hawaii in January 1973 was broadcast by satellite around
the world. More than 1.5 billion people eventually
watched "Elvis: Aloha from Hawaii" on television.

Sleeping all day and staying up all night, with his
weight ballooning, Elvis trudged through the 1970s,
giving as many as 165 live performances in a single year.
Presley's shows in these years were like traveling carnivals.
His enormous band required four private jets and took
over entire hotels. Though he never toured overseas,

(perhaps because Colonel Parker was still concealing the fact that he was not a U.S. citizen, which would have made it difficult for him to acquire a passport) Presley gave shows in large and small towns alike throughout the United States, usually staying just long enough to finish the show and head for the next city. Eventually this grueling touring schedule wore him out. With unrestricted quantities of prescription drugs readily available from his personal physician, Dr. George Nichopoulos, who preferred to go by the name "Dr. Nick," Elvis increasingly used amphetamines as a substitute for sufficient sleep and a healthy diet, and he took an ever-greater assortment of barbiturates to help him sleep.

On June 26, 1977, in Market Square Arena, Indianapolis, Elvis gave his last performance. Although he was tired and overweight, his voice was still magnificent. Afterward he went back to Graceland to rest up for the autumn leg of his tour. At last, in July, his secret troubles began to surface. Three of his old friends, Red and Sonny West and Dave Hebler, published a book entitled *Elvis: What Happened?* Their story flew in the face of Elvis's clean-scrubbed all-American image. They wrote about lurid drug abuse, violence, guns, sexual orgies, and strange spiritual beliefs. Much of what they wrote was distorted or untrue, but the book sold out instantly. Their betrayal hurt Presley. He swore to friends that he would make his upcoming tour his greatest yet, making people forget what they had read. But privately he admitted that he was overweight, tired, and sickly.

The end came suddenly, just one month later. On August 16, 1977, Presley's girlfriend, Ginger Alden, found him slumped over in the bathroom. She called paramedics, but they could not revive him. After he was rushed to Baptist Memorial Hospital, doctors said he had died of a heart attack. Later they revised their opinion, saying that traces of at least 10 prescription drugs were found in his blood, a deadly combination.

As news of the singer's death spread, fans from all over the world began to gather in front of Graceland, where his body lay in state. Eighty-thousand people passed in front of his coffin in one day. At his funeral, Elvis's favorite gospel singers performed, among them Jake Hess and James Blackwood. Movie and rock stars joined the thousands of mourners. At first Presley's coffin was buried at Forest Hill Cemetery, but later his remains were reinterred at Graceland in a family cemetery Priscilla Presley called "Meditation Gardens." Elvis's grave lies between his mother's and his father's. (Vernon died in 1979.)

In the years since Elvis Presley's death a remarkable thing has happened. Presley's fame has only grown with the passage of time. Upon inheriting his estate, Priscilla

On May 23, 1977, less than three months before his death, Elvis performs before 14,000 fans at a sold-out concert in Providence, Rhode Island.

On January 8, 1993, Elvis's fans celebrate the release of an Elvis Presley commemorative stamp, the first U.S. postage stamp to honor a rock 'n' roll singer. Millions of Americans voted in a nationwide election to help select the image for the stamp.

and Lisa Marie Presley set out to expand his dwindling fortune. They opened Graceland to tourists on June 7, 1982, and since then Presley's home has become a must-see destination for his millions of fans. Crowds gather every year at Graceland on the anniversary of his death, sharing stories about him beneath the hot August sun. They tour significant landmarks, such as Sun Studio, the Lauderdale Courts housing project, and Beale Street's blues clubs, completing the weeklong event with a candlelight vigil at Meditation Gardens.

Presley's hometown, Tupelo, Mississippi, has turned the humble shotgun house where he was born into a shrine. It sits on a grassy plot surrounded by an Elvis Presley memorial baseball field, park, and Memorial Chapel. Newspaper tabloids regularly report "sightings" of Elvis, constantly replenishing his fans' dreams that the king of rock 'n' roll somehow faked his death in order to escape the burdens of fame. Hundreds of Elvis impersonators dress in elaborate stage costumes and perform his songs at nightclubs all over the world. In 1992, the U.S. Postal Service recognized Presley's importance to American culture by issuing an Elvis stamp, the first ever to honor a rock 'n' roll musician. That same year, RCA records released a five-CD set of his 1950s recordings that brought renewed respect and attention to his early, pre-Hollywood efforts.

Elvis Presley changed forever the way Americans walk, talk, and think of themselves. The speed, the humor, and the sense of reckless abandon that Presley brought to his music is now emulated by virtually every rock and rap performer, many of whom have no idea that they are copying him. The band he put together—two guitar players, a bass player, and a drummer—became the standard rock configuration. In his day it seemed as unusual as the rest of his act.

Though decades have passed since Presley's trio recorded their early Sun records, their music still sounds as strange and fresh today as it did in the 1950s. Presley's gospel music can be breathtaking in its sincerity. The 23 songs he recorded in Memphis in 1969 offer his most mature pop recordings. Few singers have left such a wide-ranging legacy of influential performances.

During his 1968 television special, Presley told how rock 'n' roll arose out of blues, gospel, and country styles. He always understood that his work was a part of the multilayered tradition of American music. Throughout his career he strove to link the various musical styles that he loved, and in doing so he created a distinctly democratic sound. Some people call it rock 'n' roll. Elvis Presley just called it music.

Discography ★ ★ ★ ★ ★ ★ ★ ★ ★ ★ ★ ★ ★ ★ ★ ★ ★ ★

The following releases highlight important phases of Elvis Presley's career and offer a good introduction to his work:

Elvis Presley: The King of Rock 'n' Roll (RCA) (6/92). Presley's complete 1950s recordings in a 5-CD set, a comprehensive look at his early rock 'n' roll career.

The Sun Sessions (RCA) (3/76). His first recordings, all made at Sun Studio, an essential collection.

Elvis Presley: The Million Dollar Quartet (RCA) (1/90). A remarkable 1956 impromptu recording session at Sun Studio, with fellow rock 'n' roll stars Jerry Lee Lewis, Carl Perkins, and Johnny Cash, that offers a revealing glimpse at the emergence of rock 'n' roll from gospel, blues, and country music.

The Number One Hits (RCA) (6/87). All 18 of Presley's chart-topping hits.

The Great Performances: Elvis (BMG) (8/90). The best brief introduction to the many phases of Presley's career, though no gospel music is included.

His Hand in Mine (RCA) (12/60). Spirituals and gospel music.

How Great Thou Art (RCA) (3/67). Grammy Award–winning recording of church hymns performed with singing quartets.

The Memphis Record (RCA) (3/87). A remarkable studio album from his 1969 comeback, widely regarded as Presley's most mature and accomplished musical performance.

Elvis in Person at the International Hotel, Las Vegas, Nevada (RCA) (11/70). A recording of Presley's first live performance during the comeback year of 1969.

Further Reading ★ ★ ★ ★ ★ ★ ★ ★ ★ ★ ★ ★ ★ ★ ★

Carson, Lukas. *Elvis Presley.* Berlin: BTV, 1991.

Cronin, Peter, et al. "Elvis Presley, Musician." *Musician,* October 1992.

Doll, Susan. *Elvis: The Early Years.* New York: Signet, 1990.

Dundy, Elaine. *Elvis and Gladys.* New York: St. Martin's Press, 1985.

Dunleavy, Steve. *Elvis: What Happened?* New York: Ballantine, 1982.

Fortas, Alan. "Memories of Elvis." *Stereo Review,* October 1992.

Goldman, Albert. *Elvis.* New York: Avon, 1981.

Guralnick, Peter. *Lost Highway.* New York: Harper & Row, 1989.

Harms, Valerie. *Tryin' To Get to You: The Story of Elvis Presley.* New York: Atheneum, 1979.

Hatch, David, and Stephen Millward. *From Blues to Rock: An Analytical History of Rock Music.* Wolfeboro, NH: Manchester University Press, 1987.

Hopkins, Jerry. *Elvis: The Final Years.* New York: Berkley, 1981.

Jahn, Mike. *Rock: From Elvis Presley to the Rolling Stones.* New York: Quadrangle, 1974.

Marcus, Greil. *Mystery Train.* New York: Dutton, 1976.

Marsh, Dave. *Elvis.* New York: Warner, 1982.

Palmer, Robert. *Deep Blues.* New York: Viking, 1981.

Pearlman, Jill. *Elvis for Beginners.* New York: Writers and Readers, 1986.

Presley, Priscilla. *Elvis and Me.* New York: Berkley, 1986.

Quain, Kevin. *The Elvis Reader.* New York: St. Martin's Press, 1992.

Tosches, Nick. *Unsung Heroes of Rock 'n' Roll.* New York: Scribners, 1984.

Vellenga, Dirk. *Elvis and the Colonel.* New York: Dell, 1988.

Chronology ★★★★★★★★★★★★★★★★★

1935	Elvis Aaron Presley is born on January 8 to Vernon and Gladys Presley in Tupelo, Mississippi; a twin brother, Jesse, is stillborn
1938	Vernon Presley is sentenced to three years in prison for altering a check but is released after less than a year
1943	Elvis Presley hitchhikes to a local radio station at the age of eight to perform on the "Saturday Jamboree"
1948	The Presleys move to Memphis, Tennessee
1953	Elvis graduates from Humes High School in Memphis; he auditions at Sun Studio for Marion Keisker
1954	Returns to Sun Studio in January and records a sample record with Sam Phillips present; on July 5, Presley records his first single, "That's All Right (Mama)," at Sun Studio
1955	Causes a near riot in May in Jacksonville, Florida, where he is mobbed by young women during a show; signs management contract with Colonel Tom Parker
1956	Makes his first television appearance in January on Tommy and Jimmy Dorsey's "Stage Show"; performs on "Toast of the Town," Ed Sullivan's popular variety show; his first movie, *Love Me Tender,* opens in New York City in November
1957	Purchases Graceland, a mansion on 13 acres of land in a suburb of Memphis; five days before Christmas, Elvis receives notice that he has been drafted into the army
1958	After completing his fourth movie, *King Creole,* Elvis reports to Fort Chaffee, Arkansas, on March 24; Gladys Presley dies at the age of 46 on August 14
1959	In Wiesbaden, Germany, meets 14-year-old Priscilla Beaulieu, the daughter of an American Air Force captain
1960	Completes tour of duty and returns to the United States on March 2; performs on TV with Frank Sinatra in May

1961	Performs a concert in Honolulu, Hawaii, his last live performance until 1968
1961–68	Makes 28 movies in eight years, all of which turn a profit
1967	Signs new contract on January 2, giving Colonel Parker 50 percent of his earnings; records *How Great Thou Art*, a gospel album that wins Elvis his only Grammy award; on May 1, in Las Vegas, marries Priscilla, who has been living at Graceland for five years
1968	The couple's daughter, Lisa Marie, is born on February 1; Elvis returns to television on December 3 with a Christmas special that rejuvenates his career as a live performer
1969	The single "Suspicious Minds" reaches number 1; Elvis films his last movie, *A Change of Habit;* he launches his comeback as a live performer with a concert in Las Vegas on July 31
1971	Performs 142 shows in Las Vegas and Reno; the street outside Graceland is renamed Elvis Presley Boulevard; Priscilla moves to Los Angeles with Lisa Marie
1973	1.5 billion people watch Elvis perform live on television in a charity performance broadcast from Hawaii on January 14; Elvis and Priscilla divorce on October 9
1977	Gives last performance on June 26; *Elvis, What Happened?*— an exposé of Elvis's indulgence in drugs, sex, and guns—is published; Elvis dies on August 16 at Graceland
1979	Vernon Presley dies; Priscilla and Lisa Marie inherit the Presley estate
1981	A judge finds that Parker had abused his role as manager and bars him from involvement with the estate
1992	U.S. Postal Service releases an Elvis Presley stamp, the first ever to honor a rock 'n' roll singer

Index ★

★ ★

Tony Gentry, whose poetry and fiction have been widely published, is also the author of *Paul Laurence Dunbar, Jesse Owens, Dizzy Gillespie,* and *Alice Walker* in Chelsea House's BLACK AMERICANS OF ACHIEVEMENT series. He is an honors graduate of Harvard College and holds a degree in history and literature.

Leeza Gibbons is a reporter for and cohost of the nationally syndicated television program "Entertainment Tonight" and NBC's daily talk show "John & Leeza from Hollywood." A graduate of the University of South Carolina's School of Journalism, Gibbons joined the on-air staff of "Entertainment Tonight" in 1984 after cohosting WCBS-TV's "Two on the Town" in New York City. Prior to that, she cohosted "PM Magazine" on WFAA-TV in Dallas, Texas, and on KFDM-TV in Beaumont, Texas. Gibbons also hosts the annual "Miss Universe," "Miss U.S.A.," and "Miss Teen U.S.A." pageants, as well as the annual Hollywood Christmas Parade. She is active in a number of charities and has served as the national chairperson for the Spinal Muscular Atrophy Division of the Muscular Dystrophy Association; each September, Gibbons cohosts the National MDA Telethon with Jerry Lewis.

Sincerely yours

Harry R. Richmond

20 S. Betty Lane

Clearwater, Fla.

1.25

God On Trial

by

Rabbi Harry R. Richmond

1955

THE BOND WHEELWRIGHT COMPANY

Publishers

NEW YORK, N.Y.   PORTLAND, MAINE

DESIGNED BY HARVEY SATENSTEIN
MANUFACTURED IN THE UNITED STATES OF AMERICA
BY
BOOK CRAFTSMEN ASSOCIATES, NEW YORK

Dedicated to:

M. L. L.

Preface

The sermons in this volume were not written to be "a book of sermons." The writer produced them in speaking to a wide and diversified radio audience while participating in a series of Interfaith Chapel Hour programs broadcast over radio station KFH in Wichita, Kansas.

Combining world topics with religious teachings and admonitions, Rabbi Richmond is capable of striking beneath the veneer of present day sophistries. This selection of sermons will provide much stimulating reading for theologian, student, or layman.

Of particular import are two sermons, "Prejudice with an Honorable Twist" and "Applied Religion." Thoughtful Americans of all religious beliefs will read these with recognition of significant thinking on the part of the writer. Timely reading is found in the sermon on "Loyalties." The fullness of interfaith understanding and a simply stated insight into another man's religion is found in "A Jew Views a Christian."

Rabbi Richmond has been serving for some time as Auxiliary Chaplain to the military personnel of the Jewish faith stationed at McConnell Air Force Base, Kansas. Thus, for a fellow clergyman and a fellow Chaplain, I preface this volume of his sermons with the belief they will bring thoughtful inspiration to the reader.

CHARLES I. CARPENTER
Chaplain (Major General), USAF
Chief of Air Force Chaplains

Foreword

Any serious-minded reader of these sermons will discover that they are from the pen of a serious-minded author, a man who lives thoughtfully and who seeks to know the will of God for our generation. He speaks with "concern." His prophetic heart is always sensitive to the tensions and anxieties of distraught people, and it is large enough so that no one of us is excluded. Rabbi Richmond's spirit is ecumenical.

In these pages we will find some long-sought answers to perplexing problems. The author will furnish clearer perspectives and to him we will be grateful for new insights and wholesome inspirations.

We who have heard his voice over the radio will now rejoice to have his messages before us on the printed page.

Lloyd S. Cressman
President, Friends University
Wichita, Kansas

Table of Contents

Introduction

Frequently I am privileged to welcome to the auditorium of Temple Emanu-El diverse groups, representing different churches of Wichita; and occasionally church groups from towns not too far from Wichita. The number of Christians crossing the threshold of the Temple per year, in consequence, exceeds the number of Jews meeting there during the same period of time. My concern, however, is not with number, but with the spirit of "at home" that greets every group that enters the Temple, to be briefed on some aspect of Judaism, or on the Synagogue.

For always I experience a spirit of elation in welcoming a church group to the Temple. Not in telling the story of Judaism, or the tradition of the Synagogue, but in revealing to the group the ecumenical character of the Synagogue. The Synagogue, in the words of King Solomon, is "a house of prayer for all peoples." True it is, that the Synagogue abounds in symbols and ceremonies, distinctive and differentiating; but towering above the difference is the sweeping spirit of Judaism, accenting oneness: oneness of God, oneness of mankind.

This transcending ideal of unity amidst diversity is gaining ground ever more in enlightened, religious thought of today. Against the religious wars of yesterday, with sects battling each other for supremacy of belief, for thought-control, is the rewarding recognition that "in my Father's House there are many mansions." Protestant, Catholic, and Jew have learned to live together in amity in America, and to respect one another's belief in sincerity. Credit for forwarding this respect is due our expeditionary military forces of World War I and World War II. I deem it a privilege, as U.S. Army Chaplain, overseas in World War I and II, to testify that the regulation military chapel — one common sanctuary, used by Protestants, Catholics, and Jews — helped much to gain a respectful recognition of one for the faith of the other.

The tradition of "one meeting place" for the three diverse religious groups in the military forces of America remained long after the wars were over. Today, every army, navy or air-base chapel, at home or in foreign lands, is the central sanctuary for every man of every faith. The chaplains in the chapel reflect the spirit of the sanctuary in the recognition and cooperation extended by one to the other.

An example of unity amidst diversity, in the religious services of the American military forces, is the McConnell Air Force Base Chapel, in Wichita, Kansas. The McConnell Air Force Chapel is not only a model chapel in design and architecture, but in the spirit of understanding between the chaplains of the differing denominations meeting there for religious services. Worthy of mention is the "Chapel Hour" of the McConnell Air Force Chapel, broadcasting consecutively three religious services — Catholic, Jewish and Protestant — on Sunday mornings, from 9 to 11 A.M.

Some of the sermonettes I was privileged to broadcast, as auxiliary chaplain, appear here in book form, in capsule size, brief enough to be read while on the run. The persuasive behind this humble effort, however, is not brevity; though it is a merit in sermons. The commanding urgency is the hunger for understanding between man and man. At a time in the annals of man when misunderstanding spills over from land to land, and confusion nestles in the breast of man, what will resolve our complexities if not the under-standing word? Do we not say: "In the beginning was the word"?

Nothing springs into being by itself, my own efforts not excluded. It is with profound gratitude therefore that I voice appreciation to those who have been helpful in this humble adventure: the late Dr. Robert Rolofson, Chairman, Kansas State National Conference Christians and Jews, for the vision and sponsorship of "The Chapel Hour"; to Mr. Frank Webb, Manager KFH Broadcasting Co., Wichita, Kansas, for wholehearted cooperation in The Chapel Hour broadcast; to Mr. Louis Rittenberg for generous assistance in planning and coordinating work that transformed the spoken word into a printed page.

Harry R. Richmond

Paris, France
August 2nd, 1954.

God On Trial

1

Suppose You Were God

Man, ever since he began to worship some thing, or some one other than himself, ascribed to the deity he worshipped powers he himself did not possess. Thus, primitive man, sorely needing rain or sunshine, for example, but unable to produce them, began to worship them. First, therefore, to receive the homage and honor of man, to be deified by man, were the forces of nature.

The leap in time and thought between the worship of the forces of nature and the adoration of God, who is manifest in the forces of nature, spans the saga of the pilgrimage of man, in his ever-increasing quest to search, to find, to know God. Not least in man's endeavor to understand God is his concept that God not only is the Power revealed in the governance of the universe, but is the Spirit abiding in the heart of man, prompting him to seek good and forsake evil.

This inner prompting of man projects the problem of the freedom of man. For this silent prompting, this "still small voice" that says repeatedly: "Justice, Justice shalt thou pursue"; this heavy burden of conscience that murders sleep and will not let man rest until he rights the wrong — does it not rob man of freedom of choice? To modern man, in particular, this matter of freedom of action poses an especially serious question: For, if God is omniscient and omnipotent, and the will of God for man is a life charged with integrity and morality, then the moral conduct of man is the issuance and consequence of the omnipotence and the will of God, rather than man's free action. And what does modern man prize more than freedom itself, if not freedom of choice and freedom of action, moral freedom not excluded? A pertinent question, indeed, in a world battling for human freedom.

Modern scientific thought argues no less in favor of freedom of man. No scientific verdict has yet been delivered as to which of the two factors — heredity or environment — shapes and molds the character of man. If biology favors heredity, sociology, by the same token, is inclined in the direction of environment. Suffice for the moment to say that no jury will sit in judgment in a criminal case without having given primary consideration to the motives of the criminal in the case; to the environmental and hereditary factors that motivated his conduct; to the crucial question: whether the criminal acted as a sane and free agent, or as the victim of impulses and conditions over which he had no control.

The same concern about human freedom prevails in the field of economics. Those who favor free enterprise, for example, would say that in its sphere and orbit man is free to carve and create his own economic opportunity. They would point to the endless number of men who transformed, with their own hands, humble beginnings into promising economic returns. But they would be met with the argument that an economic determinism controls human destiny; that without a planned economy, man is a slave to economic forces beyond his power to control or regulate. Freedom of man, it would seem then, is limited in the fields of religion, biology, sociology and economics — to mention but a few of the many avenues in which freedom is limited for modern man.

If, in the face of it all, we declare that man *is* a free agent, it is essentially due to an inner conviction that this is true, despite all proof to the contrary. In our courts of law, punishment is meted out in keeping with this conviction.

How then shall we interpret the aspect of God's Omnipotence that argues against freedom of man? By asking the following question: Suppose you were God: Would you rather limit your omnipotence, or limit the freedom of man? When a mother permits her child to touch a hot stove, she limits her omnipotence, that the child may not be limited in freedom of action and may thus learn, by experience, not to touch a hot stove.

We are confirmed in our premise by the words of the scientist and Nobel prize winner in physics, Lecomte du Nouy, when he says in his famous work, *Human Destiny,* "God abdicates his omnipotence that man may be a free agent."

Man is not an automaton, nor a machine, nor a mechanism. A mechanism is limited in its process; man rises above his limitations. Man converts his handicaps, his limitations, into a challenge. He rises to meet that challenge with the inner conviction that man is a free agent. In that conviction lies the triumph of man materially and spiritually. And Jewish thought confirms the freedom of man in these words; "Behold, I place before thee today life and death; choose life."

2

A Jew Views a Christian

IN A RECENT contribution on "Catholic Information," the following question is asked: "Are only Catholics saved?" And the answer is, "By no means! Such is far from the teachings of the Catholic Church. The Catholic Church," we are further told, "leaves the judgment of each and every man to our All-Just and Merciful Father." This liberal view of the Catholic Church concerning the salvation of those not within her fold may also justly be appropriated by the Synagogue, as expressive of the Jewish view concerning the Christian. If necessary, the Synagogue can say it on its own authority. The Talmud, speaking of the salvation of the non-Jew, says: "The righteous of the gentiles will inherit their portion of bliss in the world to come."

Let it be admitted, however, that the talmudic appraisal of the non-Jew is not as well known as it should be. The very opposite is true. There are opinions abroad that tend to divide Jews and Christians into opposite camps, burning all bridges between them. At times, one is tempted to conclude that, at best, the relationship between Jew and Gentile is that of "friendly enemies." And wherever that is true it is due to lack of understanding of the authentic view of Jew concerning Christian.

Misunderstanding is possible for one inside looking outside. Exclusive of those green pastures where the other's grass is always more green than our own, one's own class, cult or creed is better than the other's; otherwise one's loyalty would not be persistent. For the differences between one culture and another are not viewed, though they should be, as accidents, by-products of time and tide. They are interpreted as the very essence of distinction and demarcation. Hence the birth of barriers between groups and areas; hence Kipling's poetic prophecy: "and never the twain shall meet."

The poetic forecast takes on scientific proof in Ruth Benedict's book, *Patterns of Culture*. The author is of the opinion that a recognizable condition of primitive culture is the attitude of the in-group toward the out-group in moral evaluation. Whether "taking a wife or a life," honor or guilt is evaluated in terms of "me" and "mine," and "them." Preference, superiority and safety are always extended to one's own tribe, clan or sect, sometimes even at the expense of the other tribe's life or honor.

Primitive demarcation between one tribe and another is father to modern exclusion of the minority by the majority. Today's bias in favor of one's own group, loyalty to the group's culture and mores, is the offspring of the persistent, primitive preferential policy toward "me" and "mine." Superiority of class, now as then, is fed on "me" and "mine," while misunderstanding is cultivated on the inferiority level assigned to "him" and "them."

Away from the primitive criterion of preference toward "me" and "mine" is the modern approach of equality of cultures. It stems from the scientific recognition of equality of races, peoples and their cultures. It is acknowledged that a variety of conditions and circumstances fathers the relative differences of form and practice peculiar to various tribes and peoples even as one hidden aspiration underlies them all: to live the good life.

The fate of culture is the fate of religion. In the market of religion there are those salespeople who know that the value of the particular commodity they sell, their brand of religion, derives its support from the accident of birth (having been born of Christian parents, or of Jewish parents or of Mohammedan parents), rather than from an intrinsic value unshared by another religion. For they know that all religions are concerned with the salvation of man, though differing in means and media. There are also those who, true to their faith and zealous for its propagation, behold, in the words of the Galilean, the mote in the other's eye, but not the beam in their own. Superiority of doctrine becomes their exclusive monopoly by the denial of similar values in other religious systems.

This sense of superiority attached to our own belief, and the consequent inferiority implied in the belief of the other, is a continuum of the ill-favor of the in-group toward the out-group. Misunderstanding of the out-group decides the fate and fortune of the out-group. And the decision is usually in favor of the in-group.

Fortunately, the Jew, with respect to the Christian, is not inside looking outside. For the Jew is brother to Christian. The Jew is not ignorant of Christianity; not if Christianity stems from Judaism. And where there is no ignorance, there is no misunderstanding; and where there is understanding, there is cooperation and appreciation.

The appreciation is evident in the literary legacy of a great son of Israel. Mindful of the nature and character of Christianity, its true mission and purpose, Yehuda Halevi, the poet-philosopher of the Twelfth Century, said in his famous philosophic work, *Kuzari,* at a time when Catholicism was regnant, that Christianity is first daughter to Judaism in furthering and advancing the ideals and values enunciated by Judaism. In the footsteps of Halevi, follows Maimonides, leading light of Diaspora Israel. Christianity and Mohammedanism, says he, are the daughters of Judaism.

The view of Halevi, the view of Maimonides, is the view of Israel. The Jew views the Christian as brother in the desire to usher in the kingdom of heaven on earth. What is there, for example, in a prayer for peace that is not authentically Jewish, characteristically Christian? In our supplications to the Heavenly Father, where, in what celestial sphere, are the Jewish chants separated from Christian crescendos? Is the hope for human brotherhood less sanguine in Jewish idealism than in the Christian creed? Approaching human values through the lenses of universality of appeal, we see unmistakably that the Jew lived the Christian hope long before it was crystallized into a religious creed; that the Christian practices Judaism even though it sails under a different name or color. Only those who are spiritually blind cannot see that in things that really matter, Jew and Christian are one religiously, even as their Father in Heaven is one. Long before Judaism became the religion of the Jew, long before Christianity was born, a son of Palestine, of whom we know only his first name — Malachi — sought to solve the perplexing problems pertaining to the human relationships of his day, even as we seek to solve the Judaeo-Christian relationships of our day, by asking this question: "Have we not all one Father, hath not one God created us? Why then do we deal treacherously, one with his brother?"

3

If I Had Only One Day

I STOOD at the bedside of a patient whose days on this earth were few in number. His sun of life was setting. Medical science had eased his pain but he must have sensed that the sands of time were running low. Again and again he uttered this plea: "If I had only one day."

That day never came. But I have heard that plea ever since. Every dying man, disappointed man, disillusioned man, defeated man, pleads in regretful tones: "If I had only one day." That too is the plea of those who are half dead, crippled in body or mind, crushed in soul and spirit, whose anguish silences the tongue and remorse seals the lips. And if they could speak, if their voices could be heard, what would their counsel be for the sake of that one day?

This is perhaps what they would say first and foremost: "Let not your legacy to your children be a legacy of wealth, of gold and silver, material treasure. Let your legacy be a good name, a name of honor and dignity."

Day and night we toil and labor to harvest and garner the goods of the earth. Yet not for ourselves, but for our children, who come after us. For their sake we sweat and sacrifice, toil and treasure, spare and save. To what end? To leave for them more than we had; to provide more than ample for their immediate needs; to insure for them a security greater than we ever had.

In that effort we forget the legend of Midas' touch. Midas' desire, the legend says, was duly granted. Gold, and the abundance thereof, was his for the mere asking. Even more. Whatever Midas touched turned to gold. Soon the blessing turned to a curse. Even the bread he touched turned to gold; the water he would drink turned to gold. Gold, gold, heaps of gold all about him, but not a morsel of bread or a drop of water to appease his hunger, to slake his thirst.

If gold only is the object our searching and hunting all day long; if wealth only is the legacy to our children, might they not harvest Midas' touch? Might not our children find in the rich treasures left them an abundance of gold, but hardly enough of the bread and water of the spirit to sustain the goodly life? The names honored by generations of men are not of those who left gold and silver; but of those who left the legacy of a life of honor and dignity.

They would say, if they had but one day, "Do not die in bankruptcy of the spirit."

Bankruptcy is a discrediting term, used mainly in the business world, identified with an investment that failed to mature, to yield returns, to blossom. There is also bankruptcy of the spirit: failure of the spirit to yield desired returns. For every man born of woman carries within him the corporate investment of parents, society and God. As a man advances and matures, the investments of body, mind and spirit correspondingly advance and mature. Then the whole man, an integrated personality, nature's finest creation, comes into full flower. The flowering of a man's personality is God's dividend on the investment of soul. But when the soul of a man fails to flower; when the soul of a man goes to seed, then God's investment in him ends in failure and bankruptcy. Then God, too, mourns His handiwork and says: "Day by day I waited for the unfoldment and fruition of the true and the good and the beautiful of the soul within you. But I waited in vain. Instead of the flowering of the soul I see only thorns and thistles of wasteland. Man! I had trust in you, I had faith in you, I invested in you. But you failed me. You are bankrupt in spirit."

One more thing they would say, if they had one day: "If it is true, in the words of the Bard of Avon, that all the world's a stage and man a many-sided actor, then it is no less true that conflict and contest are of the very essence of the drama that man plays in his life role on earth."

"To be or not to be," was not a question for Hamlet only to answer. No man was ever free from that penetrating inquiry. In what direction should he turn? What path pursue? Follow what star? This is man's unceasing dilemma. Conflicting passions, contesting aims, consuming desires split man apart continually. Like a boat caught in a stormy sea, searching a harbor for safety, is the heart of man frustrated by its own emotional upheavals.

Whither should he turn for the safety of his soul?

His inner better self knows the answer. There is but one better self, even as there is but one truth. And we recognize truth not by syllogism or postulate, but by the prompting of the heart. The heart knows the truth. Even so the heart knows the good and the beautiful. And if man remains true to his better self his heart will find peace and security, man's ultimate hope and prayer, the final quest of all men.

If man is a creature different and distinctive from all other animals on earth, it is not in the process of birth; nor in the many functions of life's existence; nor in the manner in which his life comes to a natural end. The pre-eminence of man over beast is in the values he creates. And they are never more pronounced, nor as significant as in a man's legacy to posterity. When we reflect upon those gone beyond recall, we realize that a greater legacy than the legacy of a good name no man can have; that a wealth greater than the wealth of the spirit no man ever possessed; that a greater possession than truth no man can harvest. With such a legacy to bestow, one will have no need to say: If I had only one day.

4 🌿

We Give Thanks

WE ARE STANDING today in the shadow of the unpredictable. Uncertainty, fear and apprehension are in the air. There is the uncertainty of economic insecurity. Heterodox economic theories bid for supremacy. Economic principles that were considered heretical a decade ago are now accepted by some as common currency. Inflation, unemployment and "recessionalism" are darkening the economic horizon. There is the fear of menacing atomic blasts that will wipe civilized life from the face of the earth. Whether we turn east or west, to Europe or to Asia, war is threatening, challenging the peace of the world. How shall we, in the presence of this world-shadow give thanks?

Perhaps by rededicating ourselves to the policies and principles of America. We are, as a country, poor in the number of years of constitutional government; but as a people, we are rich in the legacy of the Fathers of the Republic. First in that legacy, I would consider the religious fundament of the republic. It is not altogether an accident that on the currency of America we read, "In God We Trust"; it is not altogether an accident that the early form of government of the colonies was theocratic in concept and in character; it is not altogether an accident that America is the only modern country today that observes the festival of Thanksgiving. It is the natural flowering of the seed of religious thought, deeply implanted within the soul of the republic. The Pilgrims, the Puritans, the Colonists, were people profoundly religious. The Bible was their daily book; on its pages they meditated day and night; and they taught it diligently to their children.

The Bible was not only their hope and inspiration in conquering and mastering an impenetrable wilderness; it was their pattern and model for their individual, social, communal and national life. They lived by the word of God. The spirit of the time of the people and country is possibly best summed up in a passage in Washington's Farewell Address: "Of all the dispositions and habits which lead to political prosperity, religion and morality are indispensable supports."

In time, this seedling of religious idealism matured into the sturdy oak of religious freedom. If the beginning of America is rooted in religious fervor, its advancing steps are crowned with the ripe fruit of religion in action: freedom of religious worship. The religious zeal of former days would not have left its stamp upon succeeding generations, nor its imprint upon the contour of America, had that zeal become the fanatical monopoly of one particular denomination: the exclusive privilege of one faith or creed. Fortunately, there is no preferred status in America for one particular church, creed or denomination. Therein lies the greatness of the religious character of America. Religion, in America, is not a tool of the state, it is man's choicest prerogative for the voice of his conscience. At a time when Russia declares religion the opiate of the masses, it is a benediction to meet in this religious assembly and give thanks to the Heavenly Father for the principle of religious freedom in the legacy of America.

This and more: If the currency of America reminds us of trust in God, America's most distinguished relic, the Liberty Bell, reminds us of the sovereignty of the individual, the second principle in the legacy of America. In this land man is a free individual. The religious impulse of America was not to end in mere piety, in lip worship, in homage to ritual; it sought channels far deeper, in harmony with the liberating spirit of religion. Of what avail religious freedom, if man is to remain a slave politically? To liberate man politically no less than religiously is another great American adventure. It is the adventure we call democracy. On this continent the Fathers of the Republic sought to create a form of government that will safeguard and insure the rights of the individual against the encroachment of state. And our government, federal, state or municipal, has but one objective: to protect the rights of the individual before the law. In America no rights are superior to the rights of man; in America the citizen is sovereign; in America man is politically a free agent.

The significance of political freedom becomes evident when we reflect upon the contending forms of government now challenging world attention: communism and democracy. According to communism the state is supreme; the individual exists only to further the interests of the state. The individual is not an end in himself; he is but a means to the end; and the end is the state. Democracy is the bulwark of the individual. Within its orbit man is a free agent religiously, politically, economically. "Our flag," said Franklin Delano Roosevelt, "for a century and a half has been the symbol of the principles of liberty of conscience, of religious freedom and equality before the law." For that spirit of democracy we give thanks.

And there is one more principle in the American legacy

for which we are grateful: the principle of peace. Americ[a]
always sought the portals of peace rather than the ways of
war. Our influence in the council of nations has always been
in the direction of peace. We do not seek the spoils of conquest, but the peace and happiness of our neighbors. At a
time when China is annexed; when Europe is enslaved;
when Germany is split asunder; when Russia is waiting for
"the day," to marshal its legions in another World War
conquest, America is seeking the peace of the world. For
America is set against war; at heart we are a peace-loving
nation. No country on earth can exhibit an international
boundary line, as between America and Canada, and not a
soldier on patrol.

Here again the conscience of America has been well expressed by the late President Roosevelt in an Armistice Day
address, when he said: "The primary purpose of this nation
is to avoid being drawn into war. It seeks also in every prac-
ticable way to promote peace and discourage war." To seek
peace and avoid war, to be a friend of every nation and a
good neighbor to the north and south of us, is an American
policy for which we today give thanks.

To these principles and policies of America we dedicate
ourselves, no less today than in the past.

May the future not dim the past. May America continue
to be faithful, true and loyal to its heritage; to its principles
of religious freedom, democratic government and the peace
of nations May the zeal of the Fathers of the Republic continue to inspire the hearts and minds of their sons and
daughters, to the end that America may be privileged to lead
the world in paths of peace and in the ways of righteousness.

God on Trial

A MOST SHOCKING catastrophe gripped our attention recently. Indeed, the whole civilized world was shocked by the tragic news of a child kidnapped and murdered. The memory of the Lindbergh child was revived by the gruesome kidnapping and murder of six-year-old Bobby Greenlease. Our sympathy went out to the bereaved parents in their hour of grief and sadness. A whole nation was sorrow-stricken because of a treachery incomparable.

Civilized people everywhere inevitably and inescapably ask, "What is the mental climate of a society plagued again and again by kidnapping and murdering of its innocent children?"

And if this is the question hurled at society, what answer shall we give when the same question is asked, under the circumstances, concerning God, who is the embodiment of love and mercy? In the presence of a God of mercy, the sorrow and suffering of the parents of Bobby Greenlease seem inexplicable. How are we to reconcile their woe and agony with a God of love? Add to the kidnapping catastrophe the crashes and the clashes, the stabbings and the shootings that mount daily, and the conciliation of wholesale death with a God of love and mercy seems impossible.

In the face of such tragedies and their like, God, in the human eye, is on trial.

The passive believer acquits God by saying, "Suffering is the punishment of the Lord for sins comitted." Should you ask, "Why do the innocent and the guilty suffer alike?" the answer will be: "There is another world, a future world, where the innocent will receive their due reward, and the wicked their full measure of punishment."

Right opposite swings the pendulum, when we meet the unbeliever. He cannot accept a God of justice, in the midst of injustice; he cannot accept a God of love, in the midst of hate; he cannot accept a God of mercy, in the midst of cruelty. Hence he says: "This world is but the offspring of accident. Man and beast alike share the fate or fortune that may betide them. When the slings of misfortune assail you; when sorrow befalls you, there is no redress, no answer to petition. For man is the victim of circumstances, subject to accidents over which he has no sway, no control."

Between these two, the passive believer and the unbeliever, you find the man who is ready to wrestle with the circumstances of life. He finds injustice in the world; but he is not defeated. He does not reject the world. Like Jacob of old, he wrestles with the angel in the darkness, even the whole night through if necessary, that dawn may bring a blessing. He faces the vicissitudes of life; he realizes that every step of man is tracked with sorrow and suffering; but he never gives up the struggle. He battles on. Over and against the misfortunes of life he points to the blessings of life. Not that the wrestler is bereft of faith. Rather, the contrary is true. He does not take his faith lying down. Like Jacob of old, though injured in wrestling, he will not let go until he converts wrestling to a blessing.

You point to the kidnapping of the Lindbergh child and

the Greenlease boy. They challenge the mercy of God. But the man who wrestles with life recalls to mind other children: He remembers their beautiful faces, radiant and cheerful as they approached life in innocence and security. He watched them grow up, safe in the love of their parents. And he asks: Why tip one scale and not tip the other? Why accent only the misfortunes of life and not focus attention on the good fortunes of life?

We are helped to come to the position of the man who is willing to wrestle with life, when we realize that when attention is concentrated upon the self, then we find only chaos. But when attention is focused upon humanity, we find divinity.

Look upon yourself only, and you become myopic, short of vision. Engage in the quest of humanity, and you behold divinity.

6 ᕗᕙᕚᕛ

An Old-New Saga

THE FESTIVAL OF PASSOVER is perhaps the first, and therefore the oldest, festival observed by the Jews for the past thirty-five centuries. Passover is a national festival, recording a national event, marking the political birth of a people: the emergence of a people from slavery to freedom. Granted its antiquity, the significance of the festival, however, goes beyond its hoary age; admitting the eventfulness of the Exodus from Egypt, its continued observance for thousands of years is in itself an event of transcending importance.

For it must be recognized that the exodus of a people from slavery to freedom, though significant, is not singular. In ancient times, as in modern times, people were politically enslaved, and in turn politically set free. Nor is the invasion of a land by an alien people, as might have been the case of the origin of the sojourn of Israel in Egypt, necessarily new. The invasion of Rome parallels, perhaps to a limited degree, the first migrations to America in modern times, as it parallels the movements of tribes in ancient times, from a poor land to a better land.

The Exodus from Egypt, however, takes on uniqueness and significance upon reflection that the flight from Egypt was not to a better land, but to the arid wasteland of the desert. To flee from the fertile Nile Valley of Egypt to the wilderness of desert land — that is new, significant and incomparable. No people ever before, nor since then, took flight to a desert.

Should you ask the inevitable question: Why did Israel seek refuge in the desert land? the answer would naturally be: to escape harsh labor in Egypt. In face of the hardships imposed upon the enslaved by the taskmasters of Pharoah, even the desert was welcome. Even the desert is paradise if it means escape from the cuts and bruises of leather lashes. Plausible though this reason may be for Israel's escape from Egypt, a motive far greater than skin-saving seems to underlie the Exodus from Egypt.

We miss the significance of the Exodus from Egypt when we fail to realize the passion of Israel for freedom. Passover not only celebrates a most ancient festival that recognizes the political birth of a people; it celebrates the first break of man from slavery to freedom. Enslavement of peoples, subjugation of the conquered, was common practice among the masters of the ancient world. Thus the institution of slavery became the foundation of the economic and social order of ancient Egypt, Babylon and Assyria. The enslaved had no recognition, no status, no legal protection. They were outlawed; they were the property of the state, as cattle and flocks are the property of their owners. For slaves to break the yoke of the master, to seek status, to achieve independence was unknown, even as it was unthinkable.

First to break the encirclement of man, the enslavement of the soul, the subjugtion of races, was the slave-people: Israel. The slave, himself, broke the yoke of slavery; the imprisoned, themselves, broke the chains that enchained them; the tyrannized, themselves, broke the stranglehold of the tyrant, and with freedom's torch in hand, marched forward to freedom. Only a people intoxicated with passion for freedom could break the chains of enslavement and become mankind's vanguard of freedom. Therein the significance of the festival of Passover. It celebrates mankind's first break for human freedom.

Passover not only celebrates mankind's first beachhead for freedom: It rings the call for freedom today. Freedom is not an heritage transmitted from generation to generation. Freedom must be prized and possessed forever by every man, in every age, in every generation. We must battle for freedom, and be ready to die for it, if necessary, that freedom may live and perish not from the face of the earth. For there is a Pharaoh in every generation; a tyrant in every age, ready to enslave mankind; ready to stifle freedom. Our own generation is not free from it. We live today in the shadow of enslavement.

To escape the tyranny of our time, it is not enough to bask in the glory of the Founding Fathers, who achieved freedom for this land. Every freedom-loving man must see himself threatened by the inroads of enslavement and gird himself for the heroic task of freedom's forward march.

The saga of old, the Exodus from Egypt, celebrated in the festival of Passover, is repeating itself in new form, in the exodus of all who can, from the Egypt of our time to the promised lands of life and freedom. May the newly won freedom of today inspire hope in the freedom of tomorrow.

7

Report on Israel

A REPORT ON the new State of Israel claims attention. For Israel is a new State in a part of the world where nothing new ever occurs. It is a part of the world where the sun is hot, where labor languishes, where slumber is sweet day and night. It is a part of the world where medievalism passes for modernity, where the Bedouin and his herd roam over the land, where the camel's back is still the vehicle of transportation. It is a part of the world where the blowing wind still separates the grain from the chaff on the threshing floor, where disease still stalks unchecked, where woman is still the chattel of man. A report on Israel is news.

First to report is the fact that there is this new State of Israel. The accent on the word "new" sums up the mood and manner of Israel. For Israel is of the ancient world, antedating Greece and Rome, rivaling Syria, Babylon and Egypt of antiquity. Israel, it must be remembered, is the land of the Bible; the land that has remained the record of a page; the land that has become the storehouse of a Word; the inspiration of a message received and reverenced.

In the strange interlude between the old and the New Israel, the land suffered destruction and devastation, ruin and conquest, aridity of the soil and sterility of the soul.

Conquered by Rome, mastered by Islam, sacked by the Crusaders, annexed by Turkey, seduced by England is the record enforced upon it by emperors and kings struggling for the possession of a land sacred to Jew, Christian and Mohammedan.

During this millennia-old struggle between countries and kings — for the possession of the land — the former inhabitants of the land, the Jews, were lost in the shuffle. Christian or Mohammedan, as the fate of war decreed, could enter the land and possess it, but not the Jew, bereft of arms to shoot his way to the possession of his homeland. As late as 1947 the British Navy blocked the entrance of a Jew to Palestine.

Came 1948 and independence for Israel. That is the strange saga of the State of Israel.

After nearly two thousand years of death and destruction, the land came to life again in the heroic resurgence of the sons and daughters of Israel. All that is significant in Israel today stems from their spirit of independence, from the liberation of the land. The man on the street, the merchant in his shop, the worker at his tools, the farmer at his plow, the housewife at the kitchen stove, and the young people dancing the Hora, all are breathing the spirit of freedom, born of the rightful restoration of a people to its land, a land to its people.

In that restoration, in that reunion, there is rebirth and rejuvenation: There is gladness on the face of the Israeli, and greenness in the valley of Jezreel. The eternal wanderer is becoming rooted in the soil, and the ubiquitous middleman a productive laborer. The desert land is made to bear fruit, and the rocks are yielding iron and copper. At every turn of the road, every city you visit, every villager you chat with, crowds upon you the ineradicable recognition that you are face to face with Promise and Fulfillment. Israel is the veritable Promised Land. Given time and patience, Israel will be a land flowing with milk and honey.

On-the-spot observation of city and country, of village and farm, of kibutz communities and cooperative industries confirms it. In the city there is thriving commerce and stimulating free enterprise; in farm communities there is the persistent determination to make the arid land yield the needs of the tillers of the soil. In the Negev, the vast southland of Israel, in the area of Beer-Sheba, a bit of land comparable to the Arizona desert in America, you witness the miracle of conversion; a wasteland converted to farm and field, yielding satisfying harvests. Water is as scarce in the Beer-Sheba area as in the American desert, but America has other, fertile fields and replenishing water. Not so Israel. It is poor in fertile land and impoverished in water sources. Israel must make every bit of land, arid as well as arable, count. That necessity makes the arid land yield its measure by the invention of irrigation.

By the same token the Dead Sea is being resurrected to life and usefulness. Its rich mineral deposits are gradually being extracted and transformed into potash and other mineral fertilizers. More than fifteen hundred tons of potash have been exported by Israel. Of promise no less are the copper mines of the land, abandoned since the days of King Solomon. Even oil deposits are not far from a possibility. Should that hope become a reality, the self-sustaining power of Israel will be attainable in the not very distant future.

The striking difference between Israel and the Arab states claims attention too. Neighbor to Lebanon and Syria, to Jordan and Egypt, an existing cultural and political difference — more than the apparent geographical boundary line warrants — separates them. In Lebanon or Syria social life, political government and intellectual adventure are set in the frame of the Middle Ages. In Israel, save for the decided distinctiveness of the Hebrew language, the pattern of life is modern Westernism.

Israel's form of government is democratic; its intellectual outlook is progressive; its social orbit highly cosmopolitan. Israel undeniably lacks the "know-how" of American production, the industrial efficiency characteristic of America, the mechanical and technological advancement of the atomic age; but it has a compensating balance sheet: Israel is ambitious, energetic, productive, alert, advancing; eager to take its place among the modern nations of the world.

Not least in the significance of Israel is its recall of memory: Every spot of interest observed in that land is clothed with a sacredness and reverence unshared by any other land. Jerusalem is more than just another city: it is the city of King David; the home of King Solomon's Temple; the heart-throb of the Christian world. Jerusalem is the spiritual womb of two religious cultures, embodied in two sacred testaments: the old and the new. Nazareth is more than another town in Galilee; it is the place where, for the Christian, every section and every street speaks of the Galilean, as He walked among them. By the same token, the country of Israel is more than just another country. It is the world's sanctuary; mankind's memorial of the spirit; the meeting place of Jew, Christian and Moslem on the highway to the Lord.

8 🌿

The Festival of Lights

THERE IS SOMETHING peculiar to the Festival of Lights, now observed in the House of Israel, that makes it singular and distinctive; it is the only festival, minor though it be, that is not biblical. The observances of all the other festivals, our holydays and holidays, are derived from authoritative sources in the Bible. Chanukah rests not upon a biblical injunction. It is derived from the apocryphal books of the Maccabees. And there is one more distinction shared by the Festival of Lights. It is a war festival. All the other days Israel commemorates are either religious or national. Thus, for example, the three pilgrim festivals, being agricultural in nature, are unmistakably national. The two holydays, on the other hand, by their very names betoken their essential characteristic. They are religious holydays. But the Festival of Lights is unlike the other classes of festivals mentioned.

Were Israel a warlike nation; had our career been one extensive battleground; had we counted our heroes among the marshals, generals and admirals of the world; had Israel's prime possession been the sword rather than the scroll, then this festival of victory in war would not have been so lonely on the calendar of Israel. But the heroes of Israel are not heroes of the sword but of the soul. Our battle cry is Peace. How then shall we appraise the Festival of Lights, a festival of war?

Some say it is a religious festival, and the facts of the matter seem to favor them.

If the recorded data in the Maccabees is authentic, then it appears that the contest between Antiochus and the Maccabees was a religious contest. Israel was content to remain a vassal state of Syria as long as its religious autonomy was preserved. And one is safe to conclude that had the ideal of national unity, so ardently sought by Antiochus, been limited to political allegiance, and not to religious loyalty, not a finger of the Maccabees would have been raised against the forces of Nikanor. The military pressure of Syria that aimed to obliterate religious differences in Judea; the heathen altars that were erected in the Temple of Jerusalem; the prohibitions against rights and performances that were distinctly Israeltish, these were the forces that caused Judea to rebel against Syria and crown the banner of the Maccabees with victory. In brief: they battled for religious freedom and won.

And when they sought to perpetuate this victory, to accent this new birth of religious freedom, they declared that it be observed annually for eight days, in the manner first observed. It was to be observed in the lighting of candles, in songs and thanksgiving to the God of Israel for the victory of Israel. Apparently, a festival that celebrates a war which gave battle in the name of religious freedom and consecrated victory by the consecration of the Temple, a festival that commemorates its triumph in song and service to God, cannot be other than a religious festival.

I say "apparently." For there are some, and they are not few in number, who view Chanukah as the national festival par excellence. And there is much merit in their contention.

As they view it, the significance of the Maccabean victory lies not in the first and immediate cause that gave battle to Syria, but in the consequence of that victory. A war must not be appraised only by the initial circumstances that called it into being, but by the end it assumes when it is over.

Would you judge an earthquake by the faint rumbling beneath the earth or by the buildings that are upturned, shattered and ruined? Would you judge a fire by the small match that ignites it or by the conflagration itself that consumes and devastates? Would you appraise World War 1 by the assassination of the Duke at Sarajevo, by the original contention between Serbia and Austria, or by the millions killed and maimed in the consequent catastrophe unparalleled in the annals of mankind? Would you limit the Maccabean struggle to the religious protest of a priest in Modin and not to the national liberation of Judea, finally achieved by the Hasmonaeans?

When the aged priest Mattathias raised his hand in protest against the levelling forces of Greek culture, Judea was a small subjugated state, shorn of prestige and power, prostrate before Antiochus. When the wars of the Maccabees were over, Judea was a sovereign state, mighty and powerful, feared and respected by kingdom and nation.

The importance of the Maccabean wars, nationally, can be best judged by the dynasty they created and perpetuated. The Hasmonaean dynasty was only next to the Davidic dynasty in power and influence over the fate and state of Judea. And the Festival of Lights they instituted, thousands of years ago, is still linked with their name, because of the impress they left upon generations untold and unborn. Would you not call such a festival, a national festival?

What shall be our answer? What must be our choice? Which is the true characteristic of the festival of Chanukah that Israel now observes? Are we to side with Tel Aviv in Israel, where Chanukah has become the national festival par excellence? Or are we to accept its counterpart, as in current and reformed Temples of America, where Chanukah has become supremely a religious festival, which had to be rescued from its reduction to a plaything for the children of the Sunday School by the Brotherhoods of the Temples?

We shall be helped in the solution of the problem upon realization that the distinction between the national and the religious in Israel is of our own creation. The distinction between national loyalty and religious loyalty is only of yesterday. Ancient Israel knew nothing of it. Our sophisticated age created a distinction between the profane and the holy in individual life, between the sacred and the secular. Israel knew nothing of these distinctions. To Israel everything in life was sacred, for every act of life was sanctified. Similarly the distinction we now share as to national and religious values was unrecognized by ancient Israel. Religious loyalty and national loyalty were one. Israel was a holy people. Israel too was a nation. The two merged in a complete and harmonious synthesis. To think of one without the other was inconceivable.

We lost that happy harmony and it is not well with us. We lost that beautiful blend of life, hence our dilemma. We are halting on both sides of the threshold. Those who have lost the sanctity of life must inevitably hold on to the secular in life! Alas! What else can they hold on to? Those who have lost the religious character of Israel must accept the national. Alas! What else can they hold on to? Unless it is complete divorcement from their people! And those who have lost the national aspect of Israel must hold fast to the religious. What other choice have they? Unless it is affiliation with the Episcopal Church! But the Israel of the Maccabees and after knew not of such exclusive loyalties. The religious element and the national element were there, but not as divisive forces. They existed as facets in the cohesive forces of the nation.

That, too, must be our evaluation of Israel today. Our appraisal of the Festival of Lights must help us to envisage Israel neither as a religious sect nor as a secular nationalism. The one without the other spells the shrinkage, the strangulation, the ossification of Israel. The one with the other insures the perpetuity, the immortality of Israel. And the legacy of the ancient Maccabees to a sophisticated age is the high banner that unfurls and proclaims the sanctity of individual life and the mutuality and the harmony of the religious and the national values in the life of a people.

9

Is Religion Necessary?

THE QUESTION: "Is religion necessary?" carries a decided disadvantage for me. Almost everyone knows beforehand the nature of my answer! It is a foregone conclusion that it will be in the affirmative. If not, I certainly have no place on the pulpit. What salesman would underrate his own commodity? And yet I am no less concerned with the negative aspect than with the positive. Nay, more. It is because there is a possibility of a negative approach to the question that I am so vitally concerned with it.

In every American city of consequence, two thirds of the population are unaffiliated with the church. The greater the city, the larger the number of people unchurched, or unsynagogued. New York City, being the largest city in our country, will undoubtedly be classified as the heathen city of America. Russia, we know, has boldly declared against religion. In America the intelligentsia looks upon religion as an anachronism, better forgotten than remembered. *Sic transit gloria religionis.*

"Tired radicals" claim that since they have outgrown their swaddling clothes, since they have outgrown the ABC's of their childhood, they have also outgrown the fancies and fables of the Sunday School primer. They say that if religion cannot be interpreted in a way and manner acceptable to modern thought, it has no claim upon intelligence.

By now, perhaps, we should define the term *religion*. It may be defined as a happy response to and acceptance of the universe. It is man's attitude toward the universe. It is an agency that helps man to find himself at home, in a world that is peopled with forces and powers beyond his control. It is a liaison between the world seen and the power unseen, whereby the incomprehensible may seem comprehensible.

The universe, which religion seeks to inhabit and be at home in, becomes for the philosopher a subject of speculation, and for the scientist an object of investigation.

The philosophers, from Plato through Descartes, through Kant and Whitehead, steadfastly wrestled with the nature of the universe. Plato announced: To me, God is a supreme necessity. A necessity, because the oneness of the universe, the splendor of the sun, the serenity of the moon, the breath of flowers, the harmony of celestial and terrestrial bodies, the aesthetic beauty of their sum demand it. The cosmos, he would say, upon mere observation, postulates the necessity of a God behind it. Bergson says: The universe, wherever you look, is permeated with life; constantly something is being born; constantly something is being evolved. Before your very eyes, there is a persistent process of creation. That cannot be, he would add, unless there is a creative force behind it. That force he calls "creative evolution" — *élan vital,* or God.

The scientist observes the world as matter. The property of matter is inertia, says science. This book, for example, when dropped, will fall to the ground; it will not move. For the property of matter is inertia, immobility. But in the cosmos we observe matter constantly in motion. The earth moves, the sun moves, the planets move. But if the property of matter is inertia, how does the solar system have the process of mobility? Unless movement has been committed to it, it can never proceed in motion. That motion is God. Hence, says Newton: The existence of God is a supreme necessity, even as His presence everywhere and always is a supreme necessity.

Still another scientific observation is the depreciation of matter. The weight or size of matter is not constant, nor absolute. As the law in agriculture declares diminishing returns, so the law of mechanics proclaims depreciation of matter. We become familiar with the law of depreciation, albeit in a less scientific manner, when we own a car. You buy a car today. Should you want to sell it tomorrow, you are told, so much for depreciation must be deducted from the original price. For motion begets depreciation. This universe has been in motion for millions of years. By the law of mechanics, it has depreciated considerably. In consequence, it should have deteriorated; it should have shown signs of decay. Yet deterioration or depreciation is unknown to the universe. Matter in perpetual motion, defying the law of inertia; motion, defying the law of depreciation, make the leading scientists proclaim in one supreme accord that the introduction of God is a marvelous necessity.

Philosopher, scientist and man of religion find God necessary to comprehend the universe. For the layman on the street, for the man not given to meditation, speculation and investigation, God is not only necessary, but imperative. Otherwise life, for him, is anchorless; otherwise this world becomes for him a battlefield against elements without and within. But if man is to master and be at home in this world; if this world is not to be a vale of tears, but man's happy hunting ground in which to live and create, man must be related to his Heavenly Father. Anchored in the faith that he is not alone in the universe; that he has a partnership with God, he knows the battle is worth the risk.

When we ask, "Is religion necessary?" the answer *can* be given in the negative, if so desired. Religion is not necessary. Neither is a home necessary. Observe the many vagabonds, wandering about aimlessly. Is religion necessary? No! Neither is love necessary, since there are many homes that are loveless. Is religion necessary? Decidedly not. Neither is music, or art, or beauty necessary. Are there not many lives that are without art, music, and beauty? But religion *is* necessary if this universe is not to be a strange riddle, but a challenge to reach heavenly heights.

Israel leaped beyond the rationalizations of philosopher, scientist and theologian. Since the genius of Israel expressed itself neither in philosophy, nor in science, but intrinsically in the realm of the spirit, religion to Israel meant at-homeness in the universe, and more.

Israel would have been satisfied and content to be at home in the universe, if so permitted and privileged. That privilege having been denied; having been compelled again and again, and yet once again, to live in a home not his own, the problem of at-homeness in the universe spent itself, for Israel, like a wave of the ocean, trying to be at home on the sandy shore. Gradually and inevitably, speculation and inquiry about the universe, the concern of the philosopher and scientist, receded, for Israel, into the background. Israel granted all this in the very opening of his world drama, when he declared, "In the beginning the Lord created heaven and earth." A problem much deeper than the physical nature of the universe concerned Israel. The problem dealt with the moral nature of the universe.

In time, Israel learned that one man could live peacefully and contentedly when left alone, even in an unpeopled garden; but two brothers, Cain and Abel, could not live together in peace, when they had the whole world between them. Of what meaning, to what purpose, Israel queried, is the philosophic speculation that this cosmos must of necessity have a God, when man is godless? Of what avail, Israel mused, the scientific laws of motion and mechanics, when man is lawless? Not the cosmos with all it bewilderment, but man, his troubled heart and inquiring mind, became the focus of Israel's attention; the center of all his absorbing interest. Protagoras said, "Man is the measure of all things." The Hebrew genius summarized the whole creation in this cryptic phrase, "This is the book of the birth of man." The whole of creation, the cosmos with its myriads of laws and teeming life, it would imply, is meaningless without man. Man gives to the universe meaning, direction, purpose. The world, the Hebrew genius would declare, is but a hymn to man. The universe is anthropocentric.

But when we examine this anthropos, this man, what is our discovery? Peace is not in his heart; rest has left his mind; contentment is beyond his reach. Man is crushed, beaten, bruised from head to toe. For justice is unknown, violence is on high, and iniquity rules day and night. Observe the scene where "man is only a bit lower than the angels"! He cries out for equity, fairness and decency; but faces deceit, mockery and derision. Hunger, want and deprivation ring in his ears continually; insecurity awaits him when he opens his eyes in the morning; poverty closes his eyes at night; disillusion, illness and suffering shadow him to the grave. War grips the heart of nations; human corpses are fertilizing barren fields; wrack and ruin are the fate of town and city. Innocent children are torn from the bosoms of their mothers; mothers fall and die in anguish of heart; man looks to heaven and a spray of death crushes him to the ground. Whereupon man asks: Is this the world of man? Shall man sweat and sorrow, search and speculate to solve the silent riddle of the universe, to be at home there, only to be exiled and torn from his father's land, from his home and beloved? Shall man labor to decipher the laws of the universe, only to be outlawed by his own homeland?

More than once Israel faced these crises of men and nations, and despaired. When assailed by grief and overcome by anguish, Israel would ask, in the accents of Jeremiah, "Why is the path of the wicked so prosperous?"; in the words of Job, "Why did not I perish at birth?" But everlasting fear or despair was not the forte of Israel. In time Israel rose from the ruins about him and in the words of the Psalmist declared, "Weeping may tarry for the night, but joy cometh in the morning."

This crescendo of hope, this climax of gladness, is the grand finale of Israel's drama of conflict between doom and destiny. In the face of unrighteousness, wickedness and corruption, Israel clung to the belief, almost intuitively, that the world is not surrendered to evil; that mankind is not doomed to destruction; that there is a moral destiny that shapes the heart of man and nations. Israel protested bitterly and vehemently against vice, evil and iniquity; like Jonah, Israel was angry unto death, because of the sin of Nineveh; but the confident refrain at the end of every struggle, was, "I will not die but live and declare the glory of God." Jeremiah was sustained by this faith against despair and adversity. The prophet of the exile saw in the martyrdom of Israel the suffering of the "Servant of the Lord." Job saw in the tragedy of man a vision of God's moral grandeur.

Religion is necessary that we may vision God's moral grandeur in the tragedy of man. Without that vision, without that faith, man's progress is inconceivable, impossible.

Conceive the cosmos only in terms of a philosophy that pays homage to the mystery of being; appraise the world in terms of science that respects the laws of mechanics and motion, and you leave man alone, battling most desperately in no man's land. View the world as a battlefield of values; the odds favoring the victory of morals, and man is energized to battle, to wrestle through the darkness of the night, if necessary, that blessing might come with the break of dawn.

There is a moral force in the universe, says Israel, that shapes the history of races and nations and gives man his measured destiny. Fear not the raging of the tyrants, says Israel; destiny is not in their pawn. "Weeping may tarry for the night, but joy cometh in the morning."

What sustained Socrates, Galileo, Luther, Spinoza, Dreyfus, Lincoln in their struggles, in their hours of total darkness? Was it philosophic speculation, scientific observation, or the moral conviction that truth may be bent, but not broken? Religion supplies the faith that makes truth walk erect even in the face of tyrants.

Is religion necessary, you ask? And my answer is: Never more necessary than today. For never before was the moral contest so wide and so far flung as today. Greater than the clash of arms on land and sea is the battle of ideas between one front and another. The civilization we cherish, the Judaeo-Christian tradition that has shaped our lives and influenced our institutions, is flavored with a religious conception that declares man sovereign; sovereign because made in the image of the Supreme Sovereign. This declaration is at the base of our religious foundation, moral orientation, and social structure.

Against this principle of the sovereignty of man there is the new paganism that heralds the sovereignty of state. All the horror, all the terror, all the treachery that man met in the last two decades are the consequences of this pagan principle. What will save man from total enslavement in the net of totalitarianism, now spread over so many countries and cultures? Not the weapon on the field of battle. Only faith in the invincibility of truth, right and integrity, will save man from the advancing twilight of the Dark Ages. Only faith in a Moral Power that shapes the history of nations and guides the destiny of man will inspire us to battle valiantly and heroically, the whole night through, if necessary, that blessing may come with the break of dawn.

Is religion necessary? Yes, if human progress is to be sustained and increased evermore!

10

National Brotherhood

WE THREE who are representatives of the Catholics, the Protestants and the Jews of our community, now stand before you, in our plea for national brotherhood, with a sickly conscience. For, we know, had religion been a dynamic force in our lives, the appeal for brotherhood would be unnecessary. We plead for translation into action the ideal of brotherhood, because we failed to achieve this great desideratum. We failed to measure up to religion in action. The Fathers of religion practiced the ideal of brotherhood. We preach the ideal of brotherhood. Moses, Jesus and Buddha, to mention but three Fathers of religion, could and would live together amicably and brotherly. We, their respective followers, cannot find the world big enough, broad enough to contain us. Is it because we are better than they were, or is it because we fail to practice what we preach?

Hence our confession of guilt. Religion has failed us. It has failed to make us human, brotherly in our relationship, one with the other.

Confession leads to conviction.

If this confession is not to be an idle gesture, but a healing balm to a bruised soul, then let us carry home these convictions: Hate is the death of religion. Love is the life of religion. "Love thy neighbor as thyself," was commanded by Moses and repeated by Jesus. He who hates his brother, inwardly or outwardly, is neither Jew nor Christian.

We meet not only as a summons to brotherhood, but as a call to national brotherhood. We are here not only as Catholics, Protestants or Jews. We are here no less as citizens of America. And when we reflect upon this aspect of our being, our face is no less covered with shame, and our conscience no less troubled. For I am confident that had we, as citizens of America, remained loyal to the legacy of American idealism, this appeal to brotherhood would be unnecessary. I will go a step further. I venture to assert: Had we lost all religious affiliations, but remained true and steadfast to the heritage of America, as enunciated by the Founders and Fathers of America, this call to national brotherhood would be unnecessary. It is being made necessary because of our faithlessness to the idealism of America. Washington, Lincoln and Wilson, to mention but three of the Fathers of America, could and would live together in peace and harmony. We, their followers, find this broad and blessed land too narrow to live together in amity, in harmony. And here too I ask: Is it because we are better than they, or rather because we have not as yet approximated the values of Americanism?

Hence our confession: We permit our interpretation of religion to color our appreciation of America. As religionists, we believe our religion is the best, our creed is supreme, our method of salvation the only true salvation. As Americans we project the same ideology of superiority into the politico-social sphere and say to the other group: Our social stratum is the best, our cultural conventions are supreme, our standards superior. And thus intolerance and prejudice and bigotry come to infest the fragile fabric of American idealism. But if this appeal is not to end in words, if America is ever to come into its own, then let us carry home these convictions: Intolerance is the death of America; national brotherhood is the lifeblood of America. He who plants discord and disharmony in the soil of America is traitor to the soul of America.

"National brotherhood"! Two words, symbolic of two lofty aspirations. One expresses the hope of a people, a nation, a continent. The other is indicative of the noblest traditions of the human race. One we call nationalism, the other we denominate religion. To me the two are one. As I see it, American idealism is the actualization of religious idealism. For what is religion in its highest aspect, as enunciated by the Church, Synagogue, Cathedral and Mosque? Is it not the oneness of God and the oneness of mankind? To lift our eyes upward and to pronounce with pious lips, "Our Heavenly Father," and then to persecute a brother is not only a travesty on religion, but a perversion of the principles of both the Church and the Synagogue. For there is no oneness of God if there is no oneness of mankind. If there is a Father in Heaven, then there are no stepchildren on earth.

And what is Americanism? In its broadest interpretation it aims to translate the religious values of the oneness of mankind into the political terms of human equality. On these shores a commonwealth was created to bring unto all who come here, irrespective of creed, color or cradle, the blessings of religious freedom, political equality and economic opportunity. Otherwise stated, America is consecrated to the ideal of human equality. There are no superiors, there are no inferiors in the political parlance of America. If there is an American who considers himself superior because his ancestors came on the *Mayflower,* then let him not forget the American whose ancestors stood at the foot of Sinai. The difference between those whose ancestors came to America three or four generations ago, and those who came here last year, or last decade, is only a quantitative and not a qualitative difference. Both came in search of freedom, equality and opportunity. And it ill behooves those who came first to deny those who follow after them the same rights and privileges they asked for themselves. To deny it is to undermine the spiritual and social structure of America.

We must reaffirm the ideals of America, not only for the sake of America, but for the sake of the world. If ever there was need for the voice of America to be heard, the need is now. For Europe is a house divided against itself. A babel of political tongues is clamoring for authority and supremacy. East and West, to whatever country you turn, you will find opinion proscribed and thought regimented. America is safe for individual opinion religiously, politically and economically. This prerogative of the individual, this sovereignty of the individual, sacred to America, must become the gift of America to the sore spots of the globe. While elsewhere the seeds of hate and discord are being planted, let us in America harvest the golden fruit of National Brotherhood.

11 ✽

Some Permanent Values

COMING DOWN THROUGH the ages is the sound advice of Koheleth, of Ecclesiastes fame, in these unforgettable accents: "Vanity of vanities, all is vanity." And the wise man of ancient Greece, Heraclitus by name, said: "All is flux." Millennia of human experience and the wisdom of all ages confirm the former and the latter. Vanity, it is true, is the stamp of our labor, and change seems to be the only thing permanent everywhere. The restlessness of our age, the confusion of our time is due, in no small measure, to the desire of man to substitute the temporary and transient for the imperishable and everlasting.

However, though change is seemingly universal and ubiquitous, upon due reflection, the permanent and unchangeable come into full view. Every age, every generation, every individual bears witness to some aspects of permanency.

First among the values that are permanent is love. Yet not the love that is bought at a price, or contracted for a stated time. Love is permanent when it is a complete offering, one for another; when it seeks no returns, no gain, no favor; when self-sacrifice is its sweetest offering. Love is permanent when it is exalting, ennobling, inspiring. Love is permanent because it is the dynamic of all life. Where there is no love, there is no life.

Second in the category of permanent values is the home. The fruit of love is a home. Cafés have their place in life, and so have nightclubs. But the heart of man beats true when he and his loved ones meet at the family table, when confidence is shared in the quiet hour of the evening, when peaceful repose enfolds them in the watches of the night. In the disciplined atmosphere of the home the seedling of character takes root, virtue comes to flower, and personality attains maturity. Home is more than a man's private castle; it is the repository of the flowering of man's choicest spirit. In the home promise and fulfillment meet: husband, wife and children complete the cycle of universal human experience.

Man must fulfill himself to himself, to his loved ones, and to his people and their heritage: the third aspect of permanency. The sum of idealism identified with a people is the sacred trust and the imperishable heritage of its individual members. Union with a people, with its history and tradition, with its sufferings and achievements, brings contentment of spirit and peace of mind. In union with the heritage of his people the soul of man finds anchorage. Leagued with a people, belonging to them, he is no longer cut off, isolated, adrift, a heart empty and void. He discovers his place in the heart of a people that gave him birth, a name and a legacy. The values of his progenitors become his own values, and what he creates he transmits to posterity, thus insuring the permanency of the heritage of his people.

Identity with a people's heritage leads to identity with the heritage of mankind. From the particular to the universal is man's forward goal. We seek not only our own peace, but the peace of mankind. For only in the peace of the world is our own peace made safe and secure.

In the pursuit and practice of these values: love and home, identity with a heritage particular and universal, life is redeemed from vanity, and the incidence of change does not affect the permanency of the spiritual achievement. The cultivation of these values is at the heart of Judaism, and within the reach of man. The Jew is at peace within himself, with his people, with mankind, when there is peace in the world. For the mission of the Jew is peace, as in the words of the prophet: "Peace, saith the Lord, unto those who are near and unto those who are far."

12

A Religion of Holiness, Joy and Beauty

ON THE DAY OF ATONEMENT, a day of fasting and praying, a day of introspection and meditation, Israel pauses to reflect upon the holiness of life; upon life as it might be, were it not mortgaged to vanity and futility; were it not forfeited to moral depravity. On that day Israel resolves to make amends, to seek atonement from God and man, and to follow the path of rectitude. Four days later Israel observes, for eight days, the Festival of Tabernacles, the concluding day of which is called: Rejoicing with the Law. On that day the Synagogue is a house of joy and mirth. On that day the Synagogue gives evidence, by its gaiety and merriment, that Israel, the people that created the law, is also the people that rejoices with the Law. For the Law of Israel is the source of holiness, of joy, and of beauty.

Holiness, though a word occurring frequently in the Bible, is hard to define. The scriptural passage: "Holy, holy, holy is the Lord of Hosts," though often recited by Jew and Christian, does not define the term holiness. We do best, perhaps, when we say that for modern man, that which Albert Schweitzer conceives as basic in his ethical philosophy, namely, reverence for life, is basic in the Jewish conception of holiness. To Isaiah, holiness meant moral perfection; to Moses, saying: "Holy shall ye be for I thy Lord your God am holy," it meant striving for moral perfection; to the modern Jew holiness means the sacredness of life. Life is holy; no violence may be done to human life.

If the Day of Atonement accents the holiness of life, the Festival of Tabernacles expresses the joy of life. For it is the festival of rejoicing with the Law. To Israel the Law is not a yoke, a crushing burden, a millstone around his neck. To Israel the Law is a discipline, a harnessing of the impulses, a sanctification of life. Hence a police force was unknown to the Jewish community in the Diaspora; hence a prison house never existed among Jews; hence murder was unknown in Jewish life. The Law was not a dead letter in the book, but a dynamic in the life of man, quickening the mind, rejoicing the heart.

To the holiness of life, to the joyfulness of life, we add the beauty of life, as characteristic of the Law of Israel, of Judaism. And beauty is as hard to define as holiness. Yet, we know that beauty is more than skin deep. The beauty of Judaism is manifest in the beauty of holiness that abides in family life, in the observance of the Sabbath and the festivals, the holydays and holidays. The beauty of Judaism is not in elegantly furnished homes, nor in rich creations of tapestry and bric-a-brac, but in the beauty of holiness that makes every house a temple, and every home a center of love and loyalty. The Jewish home beautiful is the private sanctuary of the House of Israel.

In that spirit Israel celebrates the Festival of Tabernacles and rejoices with the Law.

13 🐛

Friendship

WHAT IS so rare as true friendship? Among the moral values and virtues cherished by man, none is so fine, or so fragile as friendship. There is love, and love, we are told, is stronger than death. But love is fierce, love is passionate; love has tentacles, all embracing, all entangling. Love is not friendship.

There is truth. And who will define truth for us? It is a task superhuman in its implication. Not being able to pinpoint truth in positive form, we know, however, its negative characteristics. Truth, we know, is non-compromising, non-evasive, non-concealing. But truth is not friendship.

There is justice, the very rock of civilized life. Civilized life is unthinkable without the solid foundation of justice; without the disciplines and persuasives of the balancing scales of justice, life comes to an abortive end. But justice, admittedly, is not friendship.

For true friendship is a human virtue, *sui generis,* in a class by itself. And we accent the adjective "true" in friendship intentionally. For there are many facets to friendship. First to be mentioned is the friendship of utility. There is, for example, the friendship of your business partner, the friendship of the merchant for those who patronize his shop. There is the friendship of the subordinate for his superior: the employee for his employer, the executive secretary for the president of the corporation, the lieutenant for the colonel. All of these and their like are indeed forms of friendship; but they are friendships bought at a price; friendships of benefit, one to the other; friendships that last only as long as the benefit received from them lasts. Friendships they are, in the popular sense; but not in the true classic understanding of the term *friendship*.

Another category of friends or friendship should be mentioned: the friendship of proximity. There is the friendship of the family next door, with whom one chats daily over the fence, or over the phone. There is the friendship that meets you at the bridge table, or at the canasta game; the friendship born of the pleasure of eating and drinking together; the friendship of your golf partner, or the man you met on your holiday trip, while vacationing. They are friendships all; but they fail to meet the test of classic friendship.

A model of classic friendship has been preserved for us in the Greek legend of Damon and Pythias. Pythias, condemned to death, was released on bail, Damon standing his pledge. On Pythias' return, in the nick of time, the tyrant Dionysius, impressed by their faithful friendship, released both of them and asked to be admitted as a third friend.

Cicero defines friendship in these terms: "Friendship should be based not upon mutual advantage, but upon common interests, cemented by virtue." And the Bible has preserved for us a noble example of true friendship in the lives of David and Jonathan. "As they were in life," we are told, "so they were in death, never separated."

In brief, true friendship is not *quid pro quo*. True friendship is not a form of barter, an exchange of gifts, a reciprocity of dinners or luncheons, or an interchange of social invitations. True friendship rests on a level above material gain, partisan advantage, extension of benefit. Nor can true friendship be made to order, manufactured to serve a purpose, artificially planned and superficially cultivated. For true friendship does not wear a mask, nor a smile made to order.

True friendship rests first on the intellectual level. It is the level where minds meet in pursuit of truth, and in sincerity. It is a search of mind for mind, free from utility. True friendship is a harmony of minds in the face of differences of opinion. True friendship exists where the intellect is the liaison that unites two individuals as one in thought and reflection. The Brownings are a supreme example among others possessed of mature minds.

Friendship may begin on the material level, on the level of mutual advantage, and advance to the classic dimension of harmony of minds. But it need not end there. Harmony of minds leads to harmony of hearts. Friendship reaches its highest level where hearts are met; where harmony transcends reason; where the challenge of the spirit is equally met. Friendship of the spirit is a union of souls, respectful to one another at the sacrifice of none. It is the friendship accented by Abraham Lincoln, when he said, "With malice toward none; with charity for all."

These four levels of friendship: utility, proximity, maturity and spirituality are more than an indulgence in semantics, an academic play on words. The levels of friendship are identification marks, price tags that tell the purchase value of friendship. If our friendship is no more lasting than last year's dress, it is because of the low purchasing price we paid for it. But friendships can be vital, vibrant and viable if the objective sought is not material gain but the gold of the mind — a bridge where souls meet.

Friendship of mind and soul is perhaps most discernible among the scientists and philosophers, among the searchers and cultivators of the arts; but no one is excluded from striving for the friendship of heart and mind; from reaching after a friendship that is lasting, ennobling, inspiring.

14 ᕽᔑᔑᔑ

What Makes Life Worthwhile?

I ASK YOU to consider with me a question one asks frequently: "What makes life worthwhile?" First in the category of things that make life worthwhile is belief in accomplishment. Belief in one's self is basic to life worthwhile. Life is not purposeless, a will-o'-the-wisp, an idle dream. Life is dynamic, purposive, creative. If our lives are shrunken; if we are dwarfed beings; if we become pygmies instead of personalities, it is because we had faith in something or someone, but not faith in ourselves.

Endless are the possibilities dormant within the human breast; potentialities unnumbered crave for realization; but they die dry at the root, because the faith, necessary for accomplishment, is lacking. Man, but little lower than angels, master of the elements about him, exhausts his ambition by worshipping at the shrine of the Golden Calf. We forget that man's goal is creation, achievement, accomplishment. Unto that end we must have faith; faith in our natural powers to achieve. Away with fatalism, checkmating human progress, limiting individual initiative. There is power in man to build, to achieve, to be creative and thus reach self-realization.

Life's pendulum now swings in the opposite direction. We

must employ caution against overindulgence of the self. Lest we become intoxicated with our own self-generating power, lest our innate capacity to achieve becomes a Frankenstein monster to our own hurt and peril, we balance faith in ourselves, the first great desideratum in a life worthwhile, with a corresponding opposite: we get rid of ourselves. Even as some lives are made worthless because they are starved, unrealized, other lives become boresome and burdensome because life is too much with them. The incessant brooding over our aches and pains, the constant reiteration of our fears and disappointments becomes, in time, a limiting power of our better self, a road-block to achievement. We become ingrown, introvert, intolerant, a closed shell, a setting sun in midday. Then no life seems to us as important as our own life; no sorrow as great as our own sorrow; no suffering comparable to our own suffering. It is then that we announce to the world that life is not worthwhile. Homes are wrecked, lives are ruined, loves are frustrated and sanitariums are filled with shadows of former selves, because of the superimportance we attach to our beings.

Life worthwhile is found in the opposite direction: in the deflating of the ego; in absorption, not in ourself but in others. Life is worthwhile when we get out of our encrusted selfish shell; when we stand on the highway of life, facing the sun in its fullest radiance, extending a warm heart and helping hand to our neighbors, to our brother, to our fellow man and woman. Translating our absorption in ourself into a pulsating, energetic interest in others, we make life thrillingly worthwhile.

Life is incomplete without a star shining in the darkway. The sun is the source of life of all things on earth; the evening star is the guiding light of the mariner on a tempestuous black night. In our individual lives, as we battle in the dark struggle for existence, we too, must have a star to guide us to harbor. We must have an ideal that will inspire us when the blasts of hate and malice sweep over us; when bigotry and falsehood check our steps; when light and understanding fade out; when corruption and falsehood hold sway. At such moments let there be the one abiding comfort of truth invincible. If faith is the foundation, then truth is the crown and capstone of a life worthwhile.

Have faith in yourself. Come what may, meet every hazard and obstacle on the path of life with faith undismayed in your power to achieve, to accomplish the best and the finest for which you are destined. Find interest in your fellow being; not as your inferior, to be sacrificed to your ego, nor as your superior, to be humbled by him; but as your equal, as a son of God, even as are you. And harness your chariot of life to the inspiring star of truth. Hold fast to truth and pursue it always. So guided and directed, you will find life worthwhile.

15

Democracy in Action

THE WORD DEMOCRACY, at one time definable and understandable, is not so easy to define nowadays; not since Russia began to speak in the name of the democratic peoples she defends. Though not easy to define, we can, however, point to democracy in action, as experienced, for example, by citizens who exercise their franchise in a primary vote, to select candidates for municipal offices. Franchise is the gateway to democracy.

Lincoln gave expression to the classic meaning of democracy when he defined it in these unforgettable words: "a government of the people, by the people, for the people." Implicit in the rule of the people — democracy — is the security of the individual. This apparent paradox, the rule of the masses for the good of the individual, is of the very soul and spirit of democracy. Accordingly, the safety of the citizen is the vitality of democracy.

Franchise is not the only form of democracy in action. Formal elementary education is another aspect of the democratic process. Elders are free to vote; children are privileged to attend school. Education for the young, on the democratic level, is not the prerogative of the children of a privileged class of society, as was the customary practice in the Old

World. In America, the public school is free and open to all children. In America, the public school is the very crucible of democracy.

Free enterprise is one more aspect of democracy in action. To the prerogative of franchise, to the privilege of education, we add the opportunity of economic advancement. The democratic process enables man to pursue and practice his skill or service to the enhancement of his economic opportunity.

The importance of these aspects of democracy in action is perhaps best proven by their complete absence in the totalitarian system. In the orbit of communism franchise is unknown, education a rubber stamp for young and old, economic opportunity locked, and the key doubly secure in the Kremlin. In the face of the promise of democracy it is pertinent to ask: Why then is democracy everywhere — and in America in particular — so menacingly threatened?

And the answer is: because American democracy today is self-sufficient and irresponsible. Consider, if you please, the following timetable. In one half-century America has grown from a national state to a leading world power. We are not only self-sufficient, but we are the hope of the world. If in the ancient world all roads led to Rome, today all roads lead to Washington. Our political influence is only eclipsed by our economic power. We have become the richest people on earth. Our movies, our production power, our "know-how" reach the confines of the earth. This power and prestige of a nation, juxtaposed against a world in abject poverty, sets up not only currents of displeasure and dissatisfaction, but tides of revolutionary storm and stress such as are now menacing the peace of mankind.

For mankind is facing today a revolution on a world-wide scale, a revolution that dwarfs the revolutions of the past.

The French Revolution, the American Revolution and the late Russian Revolution were limited in scale and compass, confined to their respective lands and peoples. The revolution we face today sweeps over lands and continents, over Asia and Europe, embracing in its sweep two thirds of the world's population. And there is a turbulent current of restlessness among the revolutionists, among the subnormal, among the distressed and disinherited of peoples. They are hungry and they want bread; they are naked and they want cover; they are exposed and they want shelter. The "have nots" observe their perpetual poverty and contrast it with the increasing wealth and luxury of the West, and they become covetous, riotous, and rebellious. They are waiting for "the day" as the invaders of ancient Rome; for a day of weakened America, when they may come and conquer, pillage and plunder.

How are we to arrest that raging madness, that sweeping storm, that relentless fury? What is the hidden secret behind the glaring fact that the Marshall Plan, the Truman Doctrine, the Point Four agencies that pumped billions of American gold into impoverished Europe and Asia have failed to avert the hate of the distressed toward America? Is it not because we have been concerned with symptoms and not with the devastating disease that holds millions in abject poverty, in blind ignorance, in unredeemed peonage, in disease of body and mind? The remedy is not in a "handout," no matter how large or generous; for that makes beggars of them. The remedy is in a radical surgical cure that is remedial, recovering and rewarding.

America's stand in Korea was magnificent. America's challenge to Russia stalled a world-wide catastrophe; but the doom is still suspended over mankind. It will continue to be, until we come to the conviction that the sweeping revolution calls for methods and measures beyond mere relief. Constructive means must be found, and applied, that will remove the causes of the crisis that is driving people into the orbit of communism. First and foremost is a sense of responsibility of the West for the East. Democracy will achieve the desired end by reaching out for closer and more practical economic ties with the submerged and suppressed; by eradicating nests of poverty; by opening up avenues of economic independence; by equating the passion of the American colonists for freedom with the yearning of the millions, enslaved and entombed, in Europe and in Asia, for their measure of freedom, for health of body, mind and soul. There is hope that an enlightened sense of brotherly responsibility will quicken the democratic process everywhere. Confirmation of this hope and sanction is found in the first recorded question asked by man. Cain asks: "Am I my brother's keeper?" And though the answer is not given, man has echoed the answer in the affirmative ever since then. Yes. Man is his brother's keeper.

16 ✍

If I Could Live Life Over Again

WE HEAR the wish, "If I could live life over again," expressed quite often. The wish presupposes that one could, by mere wishing, alter circumstances; that one could, by mere asking, amend errors. If we could only have the chance to re-experience life from the beginning, Faust-like; if only by miraculous intervention, or divine intercession, we could live life over again, the path of life would then be vastly different.

Let us observe who says: "If I could live life over again."

First come those who are disappointed in their careers. Professional men or women who devoted a great many years of youth and maturity to preparation for a career, say, when failure sets in: "If I could live life over again." For they are in the grip of a fear that they are, mentally or socially, unfit for their career; that they have chosen the wrong one, or that the world is set against them. Perhaps a rebirth would give them a new lease on life. Hence the hope for rebirth.

Not only careerists are among the disappointed. There are others who yearn for the chance to try again. There are those who have met with reverses commercially, whose fortunes have been swept away by unfavored winds or untoward circumstances. Many a commercial enterprise fails to blossom, falls short of the harvest of expectation. Then disappointment reaches the heart, and frustration fills the mind. Then the captain of industry and engineer of commerce will say: "If I could live life over again."

Third in the desire for rebirth are those maritally shipwrecked. Greater than the disappointment born of failure in a chosen career, greater than the discomfort due to the loss of fortune is the disappointment that comes in the wake of marital unhappiness. For marriage carries on its wings the promise of fulfillment, the hope of contentment, peace and love, home and family. When these promised fruits fail to ripen, disappointment sets in and discontent says: "If I could live life over again."

Underlying the yearning to live life over again is the madness of a will to have its way. Hence the will to live life over again. But if our will is not altered, our life will not be changed! Even if the impossible were possible; even if we could live life over again, if the way of our life is not changed, our disappointments would not escape us. For we would repeat the same mistakes we are heir to now.

We escape the yearning to live life over again by the realization that life, in its various manifestations, cannot be altered to suit our will. The world will never be changed to suit our fancy, our plan or purpose. If a change *is* desirable, perhaps it is the change in ourselves. Perhaps it is we who are in need of a change.

First on the way to contentment is the acceptance of the world. Man must accept the world. Man is made to toil, to labor and to sweat, even as water is made to glide downward. He who conceives that paradise can be had for the asking, will always say: "If I could live life over again." But the man who realizes that the world is here, and that man must accept it, will achieve reconciliation, and through reconciliation self-mastery, and mastery of the world. In accepting the world there is the recognition that man can master the world. He who dares not meet the world will never master the world.

Next to accepting the world comes the acceptance of mankind. If our own will and our own way must have its sway, what then of the will and way of others? Shall not others have their way as we will ours? Acceptance of mankind opens the way for everyone to his right to life and the fullness thereof. Acknowledgment that the others have no less a right to their will, to their way, too, is helpful in facing the world, and meeting life on its own terms.

Third is cooperation with mankind. It is not enough to accept life passively. Life should be lived actively, joyfully. By accepting mankind we mean to enter into the vortex of life; to share in the matrix of social harmony; to cooperate with mankind. A discordant note in the orchestra points up a player playing by himself; in so doing he creates disharmony. But forty or fifty or more, playing in unison, no matter how variable the instruments they use, by cooperating, by blending differences, create harmony. So, too, is the symphony of life. In accepting, in sharing, in playing our fitting part in the social symphony of life, life is realized, and made ever more joyful.

Man need not wait for another day, for a rebirth, to begin life all over again. Man's help is ever present. Life can be made livable, now, by accepting the world, and mastering it; by accepting mankind; by living harmoniously with our fellow man. For life is found not by running away from it, by escaping ourselves or mankind, but in cooperating with mankind. In that social harmony lies the fullest realization of our potentialities, and the greatest happiness of the greatest number.

Say not: "If I could live life over again." So live that no day leaves behind it the graves of remorse and regret. So live that every day weaves a pattern of creation and achievement, a blessing to you and to mankind.

That is the significance of the Day of Atonement. It asks for a life free from regret; for a life freighted with the joy of achievement.

17 🖋

Move Forward

SHALL WE PAUSE to take stock of the year just closed, or cast a prophetic glimpse at the advancing steps of the New Year? We are told that the wife of Lot, when fleeing from a fire, turned back to catch a glimpse of the conflagration behind her. As she turned, she turned into a pillar of salt. It is a warning to man not to look backward.

The Roman God Janus, we are told, had two faces, looking in opposite directions. The month of January is named after Janus, facing the outgoing and incoming year. Who shall be our guide in the process of time-evaluation: the wife of Lot, or the Roman deity?

The answer depends on us. Do we, in a time of crisis, when fire is all about us, threatening and menacing, turn backward, or face forward? Horace Greeley may have been the first man in America to say: "Go west, young man," but hardly the first man ever to say: "Go forward."

Across the millennia, over the face of the earth, man's halting yet ever advancing steps from quadruped to biped, from mammal to man, from instinct to reason, from reason to faith, have taken him ever forward. From the stone age, through the making of crude weapons of offense and defense, through the cultivation of the soil and domestication of animals, through the growth of cities and advancement of barter, through the revolution of industry, harnessing of steam and electric power, to splitting the atom is the odyssey of man's advance. From superstition to science, from astrology to astronomy, from alchemy to chemistry, from bloodletting to blood transfusion is the glorious record of man's mind, ever moving forward. From magic to mystery, from animism to theism, from idolatry to morality is the inspiring record of the spirit of man, ever moving forward.

The history of man is a record of continued advancement, otherwise you and I would not be here. Not that man has not been at the brink of disaster again and again; but the forward pull, and not the backward step, has ever given him new vistas to embrace, and new frontiers to conquer. The greatest disaster in the history of man was the decline and fall of the Roman Empire. The greatest frontier man ever conquered was that of the New World: America. Man survived the Roman crisis and moved forward to greater heights and loftier achievements. Man will correspondingly meet the present crisis and move forward to greater conquests, to newer frontiers.

Perhaps there are no more continents or lands to discover, says the skeptic. But the man of faith says: We have not exhausted the limit of new frontiers to be had and gained. There are the frontiers of the spirit. War is still the plague of mankind and the curse of human life. The frontier of peace must be stormed and possessed, reached and conquered.

The fear of insecurity still darkens many lives, and shadows the lengthening years of the aged. The frontier of security must be challenged, its domain possessed and made the promised land of the dispossessed and insecure.

Ill will between men, races and nations is still infesting the air we breathe. The time has come to cleanse the air of the poisonous pollution of hate, fratricide, and intolerance. The time has come to conquer the frontier of good will among men, among faiths, among races and peoples.

In that hope of conquest of the frontiers of the spirit, let us face the new year with courage and confidence, and move forward in consonance with the words of the Lord unto Moses. Facing the sea in front of him, with the pursuing Egyptians behind him, Moses cries unto the Lord for rescue. But the Lord says unto Moses: "Wherefore criest thou unto me? Speak unto the children of Israel, that they go forward."

18

Children of Conformity

IT IS A PLEASURE to join hands in this interfaith adventure of religious services shared in by the church, synagogue and cathedral. It is especially gratifying to me to share in this interfaith service during the celebration of Chanukah, or the Festival of Lights, now observed by the Jewish people the world over.

The Festival of Lights commemorates the victory of the Maccabees over the forces of Syria, achieved in the year 165 B. C. E. The commanding interest of the festival however, is not only its antiquity; having been observed perennially and consecutively for more than twenty-one centuries; significant is the fact that the appeal of the festival is as meaningful and urgent today as when first observed, more than two thousand years ago.

For the lights kindled in the synagogue and in the home, for eight consecutive nights, do not commemorate a military victory, important though it was, as an end in itself. The kindling of the lights celebrates the triumph of light over darkness, loyalty to an ideal over bestial force, freedom over enslavement. At stake in Judea was religious freedom against conformity to paganism. Israel battled for religious freedom and triumphed.

This was in 165 B. C. E.

And what is at stake today? Freedom against slavery! Now, as then, the horizon of freedom is increasingly shrinking; the lights are getting dimmer and dimmer; day by day it is getting darker and darker. A thick darkness of conformity, or totalitarianism, is spreading over the face of the earth, and the children of conformity are tyranny, bigotry and inhumanity. Freedom is moving out; enslavement fills the vacuum. And where freedom has fled, there follows the crushing of body, mind and spirit.

How are we to meet this creeping, descending darkness? How are we to bring light in a day of total eclipse? By holding aloft the torch of light through the long, black night of conformity; by kindling the lights of freedom in the face of total darkness! Liberty is not a gift of God, given away for the asking; nor is it an endowment. Liberty of man, like all values and ideals prized and cherished by man, has been secured by the sweat of the brow, by limitless suffering, by endless sacrifice of life and blood. In brief, how high do we value freedom? What price are we willing to pay for liberty?

Herein the significance of the Festival of Lights for our time and day. The Maccabees met the challenge of conformity with stout heart and courageous spirit. By self-sacrifice they transmitted to us the legacy of freedom. Let us, children of the Maccabees, meet the challenge of totalitarianism with no less courage and heroism.

The call of the Maccabees, we are told, was accented in these words: *Mi laadonoi eloi*: "Whoever is for God, let him join me." Even so we say today: Whoever is for the Lord and liberty let him join the legions of the brave of heart and mind. Arm, arm ye brave, with steadfast loyalty and liberty. Forget not that the price of liberty is eternal vigilance.

It is recorded that the victory of arms of the Maccabees was consummated with the dedication of the Temple to the service of God. Victory of arms is but a means to an end. The end is dedication to God. There is glory in the war records of America, from the Revolutionary War to the truce in Korea. Neither the wars nor the victories were ends in themselves. They were always means to a noble end: dedication to God, in the service of man. Therein the pride of victory, the joy of triumph. Whether we waged war on this continent or battled on foreign lands, as our sons and daughters battled in Korea, the goal of victory was not territory, power or enslavement. The liberty of the land, the freedom of man was always the driving force behind the American arms. Battling over land and seas for the widening horizons of freedom, may our victories of arms spread the lights of liberty, love and life over the face of the earth.

19

Facing the Storms of Life

BUDDHA, A PRINCE of India, born to leisure and luxury, observing in his early age disease, decay and death, turned against life and gave forth the doctrine of nirvana, or divorcement from life. Twenty-four centuries later, Arthur Schopenhauer, world-renowned philosopher, born no less to pomp and purple, observing in his own early life the ravages of sorrow and suffering, turned away from life when he pronounced his philosophy of asceticism and pessimism. If Buddha in the ancient world and Schopenhauer in the modern world found it necessary to renounce life, what shall we say concerning life today? For, surely, never before in the history of man has life been so problematic, so puzzling and perplexing, as in this darkened hour of twilight existence. How then shall we, today, face the storms of life?

The finest men of old, in their finest hour, sought to give answer to this eternal question: — how to face the slings and arrows of life? Job and Ecclesiastes, the Prophet and the Psalmist wrestled with this problem. For they were profoundly concerned with the why of human suffering. But it is one thing to have human agony and suffering treated calmly and reflectively, in a religious or philosophical treatise. It is altogether another matter when the bridge of life snaps under our own feet, and we are suddenly engulfed in the destructive waters underneath it. It is then that *we* cry out and ask: What *are* we? Are we only as flies, crushed in flight, or are we the darlings of God, whose ever watchful eye escapes not even the falling of a single hair from our precious heads?

Bible, theology, or the traditions that issued from both sought to meet the problem of human suffering in this manner: Unto the sinner there is death and destruction; the good are summoned to heaven. This answer would be acceptable if it were true. But it is not. It is refuted at every turn of the road. You and I know rogues and scoundrels who feast on the fat of the land. You and I know precious, saintly souls who are in constant torment. To say to the latter that Paradise is waiting for them only intensifies the problem. For our immediate concern is life on earth and not life after death.

Resignation is another way to meet the same problem. It is the way of Job. Realizing his human, finite incompetence in the presence of infinite Divine omnipotence, he submits to his fate and resigns himself to the doom that hangs over him. That way man endured submission again and again; that way too, we, individually, resign ourselves to the inevitable when we face forces and powers beyond our control. For we have no other way. What mortal man can wrestle with a tornado that lifts mountains, destroys cities, and converts homes into graves? But resignation spells defeat. If man is to succeed he must have a chance to battle in life's struggle.

The third and possibly the most popular way to meet the problem of human suffering is that which every religion

aims to inculcate in the hearts of its devotees: Faith and trust
in a God of love and mercy. To which solution I am tempted
to add a word of caution: Do not test God. The sorrows
of man must not exploit the love of God; not if God is to
be more than a coddling nursemaid.

Otherwise stated, we face the onslaughts of life with one
of three religious evaluations: retribution, resignation, or
faith. In totality they represent a personal concept of God.
It is a concept of God most appealing to most people in
most generations of human existence. It is a concept of God
most rewarding, most reassuring, most redemptive. It is a
concept of God, though inevitably in conflict with the sorrows and sufferings of man, that mitigates sorrow, not by
resolving the conflict, but by leaving it to the grace of God.

Another concept of God, less personal and more advanced, is the ethical concept of God, best summed up in
the classic statement of Micha: "It hath been told thee, oh
man, what is good and what the Lord requireth of thee,
but to do justice, to love mercy and to walk humbly with
the Lord thy God." It is religion defined in terms of ethical
conduct. It is ethical conduct pursued in terms of its own
merit, and not in terms of expectation of reward, blessing
or honor. It is religion for religion's sake, as art is pursued
for art's sake. Religion so conceived and evaluated is not
conditioned upon the concept of a God Who watches and
weighs the conduct of man and accords him measure for
measure: a merit badge — the bounties of life — for good
conduct; the convict's number — the sorrows of life — for
evil deeds. Religion so conceived and evaluated lifts ethical
conduct above material gain or fear of punishment; it is free
from the enchantment of Paradise as it knows nothing of
the tentacles of the Inferno. Ethical conduct so conceived has

but one incentive: *imitatio Dei* — imaging God, or as the Hebrew Genius expresses it: "Holy shall ye be for I the Lord your God am holy."

The Sages of Israel expressed it even more succinctly when they said: The merit of a good deed is a good deed; the punishment of evil conduct is evil conduct.

And there is the cosmic concept of God. It is best expressed in Psalm VIII: "When I behold Thy heavens, the work of Thy fingers, the moon and the stars which Thou hast fashioned, what is man that Thou art mindful of him and the son of man that Thou thinkest of him." Religion here takes on a universal sweep, a cosmic character, a dimension of mystery. Man is transformed and transfigured by the glory of the universe, by the majesty of the Sovereign of the universe. To envision the majesty of the universe; to conceive the mystery of the Creator of the universe; to catch a glimpse of man and his relatedness to the cosmos is religion in excelsis.

By this threefold concept of religious evaluation: personal, ethical, cosmic, we shall be enabled to face the storms of life. Men of faith and trust, seeking answer to the riddle of the sorrows of man in the presence of a God of love will find comfort in the assuring words of the Psalmist: "The Lord is my shepherd, I shall not want." The sorrows of life will be seen as a test of strength of faith and trust in our Father who is in Heaven. They will be viewed as a spiritual catharsis, morally cleansing and invigorating. The trials of life will be accepted as the chastenings of love, as in the words of the Prophet: "For whom the Lord loveth he chasteneth." They, so tried and tested, will rebuild their lives as they build His heavenly kingdom. For God needs men to build his world, men of courage, men of strength of soul, men of faith invincible. God, we are told, tested Abraham ten times, and found him not wanting in faith; not even when he tested him with the sacrifice of his son Isaac. In the crucible of sorrow and suffering, the soul of man is strengthened and sustained.

We move from the personal to the ethical concept of God, when the criterion of religion is not the yardstick of self-satisfaction, but a profound concern with the moral structure of society. Of a certainty there is grief, anguish and deep sorrow in human life; of a certainty no one ever had enough of the joy of life; but to focus attention on the seamy and sad aspect of life is to forget the nature of life. Life is more than animalic satisfaction, more than the lion's share of life, loot and leisure. Life is a struggle between right and wrong, a contest of values, a battlefield of ideas and ideals. Life is serious, life is purposive, life is creative, and the highest creation of man is the city of God.

As our sights are raised from self-interest to moral concern, our God concept advances from the personal to the ethical. We stop complaining against the onslaughts of life when the essence of life is revealed as a fragile fabric of moral grandeur. The religious interest is no longer personal insurance against possible human sorrow or suffering.

The religious concern is a vision of "God too pure of eyes to behold evil." Instead of brooding over life, shipwrecked man is enlisted in a great moral enterprise: to free life from the incubus of evil. Man's concept of God moves from the personal image to the loftiness of moral perfection. It is Jonah rising from a God concept to suit his personal vanity and satisfaction to a God concept concerned with the lives of men and much cattle. It is Job rising from his obsession with his moral perfection and incomparable suffering against a deity blind to it all, to a concept of God governing the universe in justice and righteousness.

The moral concept leads to the cosmic concept of God. It is a concept born of the awe and wonder of man, privileged to witness the glory, the majesty and the beauty of the universe he inhabits, as Psalm VIII exemplifies. How trivial and insignificant the slings and arrows of misfortune man must meet, against a world robed in celestial splendor. Indeed, what are the strivings of finite man in the face of a universe infinite in dimensions? And yet it is man who imparts value to the universe by his conception and evaluation of its glory and grandeur, its majesty and beauty. Against the background of the mystery of the cosmos and the power that called it into being, death loses its sting and sorrow vanishes. A hint of the evaluations of the ethical and cosmic concepts of God I find in the words of Immanuel Kant, when he said: "There are two things that fill me with constantly increasing admiration and awe, the longer and more earnestly I reflect on them: The starry heavens without and the moral law within."

History presents a record of a group of people in ancient Greece, the Stoics, ready to meet life calmly, courageously, stoically. They did not justify their lives. They recognized the problems of life, faced them and accepted them bravely, heroically. Modern man, no less than the Stoics, can meet the hazards of life when girded with faith, inspired with moral zeal and transfigured by the majesty of the world he inhabits. We master and overcome the onslaughts of life, not by railing against them, but by transcending our own limitations; by rising from self-interest to ethical aspiration, to cosmic concern. We rise by the God-given power within

us, to stand erect, to face fire if necessary, to remain steadfast and loyal to the ideal, to the divinity within us, to the
image of our soul. Then we cease to be victims of circum-
stance, puppets in someone's power. We become sovereign
of our soul.

20

A Philosophy of Life

I WAS ASKED recently the following question: "What is your philosophy of life?" Perhaps you have been asked the same question. The answer is as variable as man's outlook upon life. According to the specific problem man faces, so will be his philosophy of life. Peculiar to most of us, however, is the problem of adjustment to life.

How to be at peace with himself and with the world is man's perennial task. If but one race peopled this earth, if nations were not competing one with the other for the food and wealth of the earth, no wars would follow and no spoils would be divided. But the appearance of many nations on a limited area, with limitless hunger for power and dominion, creates a grave international problem. The intermingling of millions of individuals, possessed of the same desires, in search of the same satisfactions, projects a problem of adjustment. It is then that we ask how to get on. It is then that we reach out for a philosophy of life that might enable us to be at peace with ourselves and with our fellow man.

The philosophy of life we would suggest may be expressed in these words: "So act as to evoke the spirituality of the other." This philosophy of life presupposes that there is a spiritual element in man. Some question it. Others deny it.

Of experience I am persuaded in the belief that there is a spiritual element in man. Hence my appeal: "So act as to evoke the spirituality of the other man." The evil of the world we know. The animal in man meets us at every turn. But the spiritual in man we must know no less. Though less evident in actuality it abides in him in potentiality. Our relationships to man should be of such a nature as to evoke the finest elements within him, that the spiritual force might become dominant and decisive.

The evocation of the best in the other presupposes the manifestation of the best within ourselves. We cannot expect the evocation of the best in others, if we have not first displayed it ourselves. The perfume of our own soul must be liberated first, that it may in turn bring forth the aroma of another soul. For that is indeed what our bodies are: vessels that contain precious perfume. And the relationship of man to man must be that of cause and effect; the effect being the outpouring of the finest spiritual element within others, caused by the projection of our own better self into the scale of human relationships. Hence our philosophy of life: "So act as to evoke the spirituality of the other man."

If it were as easily done as said, the matter would end right here. But is it?

Suppose you are confronted with this situation: You render someone a good turn without the expectation of any return. But when you run into the man a day or two later he hardly knows you. Even more, he ignores you intentionally. He slights you at every chance he has. What should be your reaction to him? Under such circumstances the temptation is to give insult for insult, to act as acted upon. For the best way to bring a man to his senses is to give him a dose of his own medicine. . . .

And yet, "act as you are acted upon," though apparently

justifiable, is not commendable. Because its primary concern is Self. Its guiding principle is self-seeking and not other-seeking. And a philosophy of life that rests upon the basis of self-satisfaction inevitably leads to self-destruction. For it leads to cultivation of vengeance and hatred; it causes a shrinking of the personality, and an enlargement of the ego; it brings about a detachment from others and an absorption in one's own self. In brief, traced to its logical conclusion, "act as you are acted upon," becomes self-destructive, and inimical to the best interests of society.

But "act so as to evoke the spirituality in the other man," has for its primary concern the interest of the other first, even his spiritual interest. Life is achieved and advanced not at the expense of others, but by the promotion of the good of others; especially when it is a spiritual good. For that is the greatest good possible. When we view another as a spiritual being we never use him as a tool to our service, or as a toy for our pleasure. A man who sees in another the depository of a spiritual essence will never imprison him in a sweat shop, to swell his own assets. A man who sees in woman the stamp divine will never abuse her.

The more we estimate others as spiritual beings, the more we are helped to find our own place in the world, which is the primary function of a philosophy of life. It is, as we stated at the beginning, an agency of adjustment. When we see mankind as spiritual atoms, we cease to be aliens in the world, and we cease to see in the other our mortal enemy. We become partners in a great enterprise which has for its goal spiritual ascendency. We are at peace with the world and with ourself. For we have found our place and our work. Our relationships with one another are not menaced but helped when we learn so to act as to evoke the spirituality in the other man.

21 🙢

The Quest of Man

HOW UNLIKE is man to all the living things about him. There is hardly a home where children have not one animal or another as their plaything; hardly a farm without livestock; hardly a forest without wildlife. To all of these living things, man is unlike as an apple to a stone. Though man is scientifically classified within the category of mammals, he is as unlike the variety that inhabits the barnyard or fills the forest, as black is unlike white. The potential that separates man from all other living things is the attribute of reason. By virtue of reason man is king of all living things.

The gift of reason did not come to man full-flowered, highly developed, complete. When reason supplanted instinct and how the transfer was made; when conscience was born and how matter gave birth to mind no one knows. Apparently no one witnessed the blessed event, or recorded the transforming experience. This much, however, we do know: Reason, ever since its nascent day, when yet very feeble and inert, possessed a distinguishing quality and character, the quality and character of a spade: digging, searching, questing. Ever since then the supreme occupation of man has been questing, searching, probing, seeking the unknown.

The explorer comes first to mind when one thinks of man

seeking the unknown, the undiscovered. For ever since man came down from the treetops and began to walk erect, he began to search and explore the face of the earth for more room and space, as his dwelling place. From the Phoenicians through the Greeks, through the Norsemen and the Vikings, to Columbus and Magellan, to the contemporary explorer of the Amazon jungle land, to the conquest of Mt. Everest, the saga of man has been exploration and discovery of unknown lands and waters.

Standing opposite the explorer is the archeologist. The explorer seeks the unknown, the new, the undiscovered; the archeologist seeks the past, the dead, the ruins of a former age, the remains of a civilization long extinct. One motive dominates the explorer and the archeologist: both are seeking, searching, questing the unknown. The devotion of the scientist is but another phase in the grand panorama: the quest of man. Turn, if you will, to astronomy or chemistry, to psychology or physiology, to medicine or atomic research, and you will find one dynamic underlying all scientific labor: searching, seeking, questing the unknown in one realm of nature or another. For that is the nature of reason: to dig, to search, to discover, to uncover the unknown, the better to harness its power to the use and advantage of man.

A searching of a character altogether different and distinct from the aforementioned is the searching of man beyond the realm of nature; the questing of man for God. Primitive man mastered the earth and cultivated its soil; tamed the animals and harnessed them; sharpened the stone and forged a weapon for battle against man or beast; but he was conscious at all times of a power greater than his own in whose presence he was helpless and powerless. The crops he planted and hoped to have as food during the winter would shrivel up and die without rain. How could he get rain if not to deify rain, to pray to rain and to propitiate rain, in one magic rite and ceremony or another? A storm would come and knock down everything full grown; a disease would infest the earth and kill the herd. How could primitive man stop the storm or halt the pestilence if not by deifying the storm or propitiating the angel of death? Thus primitive man deified the forces of nature, invented magic formulas, and sought, by propitiatory measures to bend the will of the gods to his favor and advantage. From primitive animism to rational deism, to ethical monotheism, is a span of millennia, pointing up man's supreme adventure: searching, seeking, questing God.

Moses spells out the eternal quest of man in his passionate plea: "Pray, let me see Thy face, that I may know Thee," and the answer comes to him: "No one can see my face and live." The Psalmist cries out in unforgettable accents: "My soul thirsteth for God, for the living God; when will I come and behold the face of God?" And Job sums it up when he asks: "Canst thou by searching find God?" And today, as in the time of Job, the answer is not in the affirmative. The finite cannot embrace the Infinite. And yet, yea, in the very face of it, man continues to search, seek and quest God, and will continue until the very end of human life.

Though not permitted to see the face of God, man divined the attributes of God and gave utterance to them in these words: "The Lord, the Lord God is merciful and gracious, long suffering and abundant in goodness and truth; keeping mercy unto the thousandth generation, forgiving iniquity, transgression and sin."

Beyond imaging the attributes of God comes the desire of man to imitate God, even in the words: "Holy shall ye be for I, the Lord your God am holy."

22 ❧

The Quest for Certainty

THE WILD ANIMAL is endowed with senses sharper than those of man. He is endowed with a keener sense of smell; he senses danger more acutely than man; his senses guide him in the selection of food more beneficially than they do man. This peculiar advantage of the animal is his distinctive heritage as a creature that lives by instinct.

But man, part animal and part human, has, in the course of his evolutionary advancement, traded much of instinct for a little of reason. Hence the name *Homo sapiens,* a man of wisdom. By the stepping stones of reason, man slowly mastered his terrain, transformed jungle land into a civilized domain, and snatched the kingly crown from the head of the lion. For the lion is king in the jungle; but in the civilized world, man is king, and the lion does man's bidding in the circus tent.

The acquisition of reason did not denude man of his elemental needs, nor strip him of his primary wants. Man is still hungry for food. Man, like animal, still roams over the green pastures of the earth, seeking food, hunting for bread. The methods of man, it is true, are different from those of animal. The animal kills; man buys and sells, bargains and barters, deals and trades.

Rising above the level of instinct, partaking more of the element of reason, is man's want and satisfaction in shelter. The lion may have his lair, the bear his cave, and the fox his hole, but man's ingenuity moved him from protecting rock and cave to sheltering home and hamlet. Man gives evidence of a purely rational element by his want of and satisfaction in raiment. For man is the only animal that seeks garments to cover his nakedness. Add one more want, and the catalogue of man's primary wants is complete: It is the want and need of man for a mate. Man's biological function is met and satisfied in his mate.

These four primary needs of man are broadly hinted in the story of the first man, in the first Book of the Bible. Adam's want of food was provided in the fruit of the tree of Life; protection he had in the shelter of the Garden of Eden; Eve met his biological needs; and raiment was tailored for him by the Lord Himself after innocence had departed from him.

We move beyond the primary needs when we meet satiety and satisfaction in them. There are diminishing returns in physical needs, after we have a fullness of them. No one can eat more than one meal, at one time; nor be sheltered in more than one house, at one time; nor be clothed in more than one suit, at one time. Beyond satisfaction of the basic needs comes the desire of man for an extension of physical wants into emotional desire and fulfillment. Not physical wants, but personality response becomes our quest. We move from self-interest to interest in others; from self-advancement to the advancement of others; from immediate personal interest to a profound concern for the future of mankind. The world becomes our home, every man our brother, and the good of all our goal and destiny. It is altruism on the highest level.

Man's ever-widening horizon, the extension of the self beyond the interest of the self, must have rootage, depth and anchorage. It must rest on and be linked with the immutability of an ideal that is authoritative, persuasive and supreme. Man's acts must be geared to a loyalty of values that commands allegiance even at the cost of self.

Man advances beyond the reasonableness of altruism when he is quickened by the ideals of Truth, Love and Righteousness; when the pains of society, its sorrows and sufferings are his own; when he cries out in bitter anguish: Why do the wicked triumph? Why are the righteous crushed? Then he will not rest until Truth breaks forth, Love triumphs, and Righteousness is on the highway.

Beyond the evils of the world, beyond the domain of religious values that would right the wrongs of society, remains the quest of man for certainty. Above man's hunt for the security of elemental needs, above his desire for a world at peace, comes his quest for an understanding of the nature of the universe, and his place in the universe. Man still seeks an answer to three questions: Whence? When? Whither? Is the universe an accident, man a foundling, dropped at the doorstep of the universe, or is man related to Someone Who Cares? Is man but dust, dust and no more? If so, what transforms dust into a power that counts the stars in their constellations? Man in his search for understanding of the universe, man reaching out for certainty, man seeking God is at his noblest. The Jew expresses this noble quest of man in the words of the Psalmist: "As the hart panteth after the water brooks, so panteth my soul after Thee, O God . . . When shall I come and appear before God?"

23.

The Quest for Happiness

WHEN THE CHRISTMAS rush is over, and gift buying tension is beyond us, the time to relax has come, and we are, perhaps, in the proper mood to consider the nature and texture of happiness. Surely, no one will gainsay that happiness is our constant quest; the everlasting pursuit of man. For no one, it seems, ever had enough of happiness, even as no eye ever had enough of seeing.

The irony of the matter is apparent when we try to define happiness. Wanting happiness, desiring it above all else, we are hard pressed when we attempt to define the term. We are like a blind man, groping in his darkness, touching things, yet knowing not what he touches; like the thirsty man in the desert, reaching out for water, only to discover a mirage. Even so is our chase for happiness; the effort to define it ends in disillusionment. For we know not what happiness is.

Happiness, first and foremost, cannot be had by a conscious, deliberate, or determined effort to acquire it, or to possess it. Happiness is not a commodity, to be purchased at a price. Happiness, like health, is not obtainable in the mere pursuit of it. We are healthiest and happiest, perhaps, when least conscious of it; latest psychological research affirms this. It is for this reason that excessive indulgence in the pleasure of the senses, excessive enjoyment of the sensuous, is not necessarily the way to happiness.

No doubt, physical maturity of body, the craving of the senses, have their claim upon fulfillment and satisfaction. This is why we say in the youth of life: "What can there be better than wine, women and song?" But while momentary pleasure there may be in the explosion and exploitation of youth, happiness does not lie that way. It is true that at times we empty the cup of pleasure, drain it to its very dregs, and while in that state of intoxication, are led to believe that we drink of the fountain of happiness. But when the heat of passion is done with, and cold reason takes over, there follows an awakening that belies happiness. There follows revulsion of body and remorse of soul.

Nor is happiness to be found in the accumulation of wealth. There are those who worship at the shrine of the Golden Calf, and wealth is their supreme asset. They have the golden touch, and their fingers convert everything into gold. Their life span is a record of indefatigable zeal, devoted to the accumulation of fortune. But fortune does not buy happiness. The testimony of many men of wealth bears witness to the fact that material wealth does not yield the secret of happiness.

Nor is happiness found in the acquisition of power. Most beguiling, most seductive is the wish for power. In the possession of power, whispers ambition, every desire finds fulfillment. Love, fame, fortune, all surrender to the controlling hand of power, says the voice of the siren. For power is the magnetic attraction that controls all, masters all, rules all. So lured, who would not be tempted by the persuasions of power? Yet happiness does not come with the possession of power. Unbridled power is self-defeating; and the greater the power, the greater the defeat of its possessor. Consider the men who attained the zenith of power: Alexander and Caesar in the ancient world; the Kaiser, Mussolini and Hitler in our own time. Men of the highest power they were; but happiness was not theirs.

Where, then, *is* happiness? you ask.

Not in external possessions, but in the inward self, is the answer. Man is happy when he transcends himself. When we move from self-interest to interest in others we are on the road to happiness. We are happy when we are caught by an ideal, when we are attracted by a value, when we are the servants of a great commanding cause.

One need not be a saint or savior to attain inner happiness. Helen Keller, a blind, deaf, mute woman found happiness in giving happiness to those who, like herself, are blind, deaf and mute. Florence Nightingale found happiness in serving the maimed and wounded. Henrietta Szold found happiness in serving the sick, the landless and homeless. In brief, happiness is found when man loses himself in mankind. Even as Joseph of old: he found contentment, gold and power, as viceroy in Egypt, not by seeking self-interest but the interest of others. Upon being asked: "What seekest thou?" Joseph answered: "I seek my brethren."

24

Applied Religion

THE PERIOD OF COURTSHIP is the finest prelude to matrimony. It is a period of romance, enchantment, and ecstasy. It is a period when friendship flowers into romance, when romance blossoms into love. Courtship is desirable most, however, in its practical aspect: courtship offers the girl, loved and enthralled, a chance to see and observe how the man she is to marry lives and has his being. For married life is more than a period of courtship. Life has its strain and stress, situations and circumstances most trying and troubling. Life has periods when love is cruelly tested. Love then is not courtship alone; but love lived, love applied, love in practice.

Even so is religion.

There is a period in the life of the individual, when first exposed to religion, that takes on the contour of courtship, and is etched with pageantry, beauty, and enchantment. It is a time when religion is romantic, magical, mysterious. But religion does not end there. All of that and more is but a prelude to religion. Religion is best evaluated not in theory but in practice; not in piety but in action; not in ceremony but in deed. Religion is what you do with your life; what you do with the life of your neighbor; what you do with the living, throbbing, pulsating world about you. So viewed, religion is not the letter of the law; it is the spirit of the law, as applied to life, or if you will, applied to human relationships.

A familiar passage in the Bible should help us to understand the significance of applied religion. We are commanded to love God in these words: "Thou shalt love the Lord thy God with all thy heart, with all thy soul and with all thy might." No doubt many profess their love of God most piously, most passionately, most persuasively. If love of God by profession of lips were all that love of God truly implies, nothing else would be necessary, and this, our world, would indeed be Paradise. But love of God does not end with a lip formula. Love of God is tested by what man does with his love for man.

Can we love God and hate man? Can we love God and practice iniquity? Can we love God and live a lie? The man who loves his mother will do nothing to disgrace or dishonor her; he will do everything possible to bring her grace and dignity. Yet the same man may profess love of God and commit every crime on record; a record that dishonors his Father in Heaven.

Responsible for this incongruity in religion is the disparity between profession and practice. Religion is still, to too many, alas! a conventional form, a traditional habit, a routine performance. It is still possible for the same people to assume religious leadership in a group, and to lead in a race riot. It is still possible for the same people to claim religious fellowship in the circle, and to kindle the fiery cross of the Ku Klux Klan. It is still possible for the same people to claim loyalty to religion, and to deny a Korean war hero burial in an American cemetery, because he was a Mexican.

It is this double standard of religion — one form of profession and another form of practice — that has tended, more than aught else, to discredit religion in our time and day. If the youth of our land finds religion uninteresting; if the scientist is divorced from religion; if the intellectuals of our time find religion unappetizing, it is because the biting teeth of protest and practice, the very essence of religion, have been knocked out of religion; and all that remains of it is a confirming echo of the status quo.

Isaiah the Prophet could be accepted as the expert interpreter of religion; religion that penetrates and permeates life; religion that is one in profession and practice. His words should help us to understand the meaning of applied religion. On a day observed by the people as a religious fast day, he asks the following question: "Is such the fast day I have chosen — to bow down his head, to spread ashes under him? Is not this the fast I have chosen? To loose the fetters of wickedness — and to let the oppressed go free? Is it not to deal thy bread to the hungry, to bring the poor to thy house? When thou seest the naked that thou cover him, and that thou hide not thyself from thine own flesh?"

If religion is to have meaning in our day; if society is to be saved by the persuasives, disciplines and sanctions of religion, there must be no disharmony, no double standard, between religion and life. In the oneness of religion and life is the significance of applied religion. There is but one totalitarianism that I accept: the totalitarianism of religion. It is not a totality that is limiting, crippling, enslaving man. It is rather a totality that ennobles, enriches, enhances human life. It is a totality that sanctifies everything it touches in human experience: the economic, the social, the educational. It is the totality that the Greek envisaged in the triad: the true, the good and the beautiful; and the Jew, in the words: "Ye shall be perfect with the Lord your God."

25 🙂

Prejudice with an Honorable Twist

NOT LONG AGO, while in the company of friends, my attention was drawn to a problem discussed in the best of families: the problem of prejudice. I was particularly interested in the fact that prejudice, apparently, engaged the attention of all present; that no one considered himself free from it; that everyone admitted his prejudice against someone or some thing; that prejudice, admittedly, was as common and current as the air we breathed. Most singular is the peculiar twist given to prejudice by forcing a nodding, conforming answer to a tortured question: "Each one of us has a prejudice. Don't you?"

This new and honorable twist to prejudice is not only an attempt to silence criticism, to upset the apple cart of the challenger, to turn tables on the free minded; but to whitewash what is dirty and ugly, to turn lily-white what is pitch black, to convert falsehood into truth. With a slight turn of the tongue, prejudice becomes the honorable practice of the best families. "We all have our prejudices. Don't you?" says the honorable man.

This twist to the negative, moreover, is more than an attempt to robe infamy with a cloak of nobility. By posing the question: "Don't you?" prejudice need no longer be in hiding, under cover, on the defensive. Prejudice, by a peculiar twist, takes the offensive, becomes the life of the party, enshrined in the best homes. "The best people have their prejudices. Don't you?" says the man robed in saintliness.

What of me? I asked myself. Do I entertain prejudice? The question lingered with me for quite a while, and I must admit, upon reflection, that I have my prejudices, and here they are: I am prejudiced against bigotry, dishonesty and falsehood. I am prejudiced against terror, treachery and tyranny. I am prejudiced against evil in any form or manifestation, against slavery of body or mind, against ignorance, wherever found. In these prejudices I am not alone; I share them with all who aspire to decency in human life. These prejudices, I am confident, give offense to no one, slight no one, defame no one.

The total effect of these prejudices is more than a negation of defamation. The effect is, as it must be, and as every man's prejudices should be, a sweep in the positive direction. Prejudice that tends to defame or degrade character or personality — of a man or a group — is myopic, short of vision, blind to the possibility of man. Prejudice slanted in a positive direction denies an organic, defective, degrading differential in man, or in a group of men, of the human family. Prejudice against ignorance aims to liberate man from the fetters of superstition, and to give him a place in the sun. Prejudice against bigotry is set against the virus of a poisoned tongue, a malicious mind, a heart of stone; to the end that man may be the master of all he surveys, captain of his soul and destiny. To think otherwise, to act in a manner that offends the human personality, is to betray immaturity of mind. As a child clings to his toys, the immature mind hangs on to its poisoned prejudices. This and more: a poisoned mind betrays a lack of mind. In the absence of judgment there is a vacuum, which is filled with prejudice. In the absence of love, there is a void, which is filled with hate. In the absence of understanding, there is an emptiness, which is filled with ignorance.

I am set, moreover, against prejudice with an honorable twist because it is anti-democratic. In a democracy, as in a human family, there are no superiors or inferiors; there are only equals. In this day of world tension, it is particularly timely to realize that in a democracy we deal with people, with citizens of the state, and not with Jews or Gentiles, with Catholics or Protestants, with whites or blacks, with poor or rich. It is also timely to realize that the vices of a people are balanced by its virtues; that even as no man is wholly perfect, no man utterly imperfect, so no people is wholly virtuous, no people wholly vicious; the good and the bad are found in all peoples, in all men, in every man.

It is this democratic approach to prejudice, which is no less the Jewish approach, that enables me to say, though stemming from the "Chosen People," with complete fidelity to Israel, that the Jew is not superior to any other people. By the same token, I maintain that no people is superior to another people. Though faithful to Judaism, I confess that every religion has its place and purpose in society, if it serves the people well. Though proud of my heritage and of the contribution of the Jew to the culture of mankind, I confess nonetheless, that other peoples and other cultures have equally contributed to the enrichment of the world. For in the family of our Heavenly Father there are neither darlings nor stepchildren, but only human beings, reflecting His divine image. I am fortified in this evaluation by the words of the prophet: "Have we not all one Father? Hath not one God created us? Why do we deal treacherously every man against his brother?"

26

America in the Light of Europe

ONCE MORE THE INTERNATIONAL horizon is cloudy; once again the political forecast is unpredictable. Again statesmen proclaim to parliaments the imminence of war; again quasi war measures are being passed by huge majorities. Once again the air is pierced with fears and threats; once again mankind everywhere is in mortal fear of the fatal hour that will sacrifice millions of human lives to the madness of hate and war. Again the threat of international conflict now gripping Europe is also manifest in America. But there is this difference: Over there the escapees from the orbit of the iron curtain seek asylum in America. Over here the citizens are pursuing their daily tasks under the canopy of peace and freedom.

This distinguishing difference should enable us to appraise America in the light of Europe. Yet not with arms akimbo, laughing at the plight of the mother country. We seek to evaluate the moral role of America in the family of nations, that America might become more meaningful to Americans. Observing the political convulsions of Europe on the one hand: the flight of courage and the disappearance of fortitude; the death of international covenants and the end to honorable commitments, and on the other hand, the high regard America pays to international agreements, one cannot help pause and reflect upon the role of America in the light of Europe.

To the degree that America shared in the framing of the Versailles Treaty of peace, America shares in the responsibility not only for the seeds of the Munich Pact, implanted in the Versailles Treaty; but for World War II, the inescapable offspring of World War I. But that is not the complete record of America in World War I. The achievement of the Versailles Treaty was the emergence of the World Court and the birth of the League of Nations, children of American idealism. For the role of America in international conclave has been moral integrity, international solidarity, and human equality.

If America fathered the League of Nations, it has no less sired the United Nations. If the world was shocked, in the early day of Hitler's invasion of Europe, by the alliance of Hitler and Stalin, America was bewildered by the absorption of China in the Russian orbit. Not only has Russia advanced militarily in gigantic strides in Europe and in Asia, but America has retreated on every front where Russia advanced. Of this retreat, the Korean War is the best example.

The concern, however, is not over loss of land in the theater of war. The concern is over loss of ground in the contest of ideas. In the ideological contest between Americanism and communism, communism is inching its way forward. We are facing an ideological war now as in the days of Hitler's nazism, with this added handicap: A pact between communism and nazism, though at first implacable foes, warring each against the other, was, nonetheless, basically quite logical. A pact between communism and democracy is a monstrosity. For while there is a common denominator to fascism, nazism and communism, expressing itself in the ideological trinity of supremacy of state, supremacy of blood and supremacy of leader, *Führer,* or commissar, democracy declares the equality of states, races, and men. In America no right exists superior to the rights of man; no force exists stronger than the soul force of man; no power more dominant than moral power.

Because communism and nazism are the obverse and reverse of the same coin, there is much reason for the fear that has gripped mankind East and West. For the ever increasing orbit of communism is not in the power of armies to check or to stop. A new pattern of society, tailored to Marxian fashion, is emerging. When it arrives (not the atomic bomb), it will black out all traces of civilization, culture and freedom known to man. The world crisis today is in the sweep of totalitarianism over Europe, the Mediterranean basin, and the East. Already the Kremlin insists upon a seat for China in the U. N. In time, it will not insist; it will have it. Then the fate of Formosa will be the fate of Korea, the fate of Poland, Austria, Czecho-Slovakia, Hungary and Rumania. Italy and Turkey will be, perhaps, next swept into the orbit of communism. Then freedom will be gone; culture will live in memory; and religion be a mockery.

America, sensitive to the peril in the Soviet sweep, must be concerned evermore with the safeguards of democracy. The Russian-Chinese alliance should have a sobering effect on America. We have been awakened to the evil of propaganda; we have discovered the falsehood underlying the seductive, serpentine words: "peoples' democratic nations." We know now, as never before, that Italy is not fighting communism. We know now, as never before, that Japan is not fighting communism. We know now, as never before, that the barrages and explosives against communism, advanced by one group or another, in the name of pure Americanism, pure democracy, are but decoys, to deceive and detract from the real and alarming danger, lurking behind the net of communism. The realization of the peril waiting in ambush; the quickening of the American conscience in defense of democracy, cannot come too soon for the safety of America, for the salvation of mankind.

Ready to defend America; to defend freedom-loving people everywhere, America has been neither belligerent nor bellicose. Nor was the American price of peace territorial expansion, or acquisition of land. "Fourteen points" was all we asked as the price of peace in World War I. Woodrow Wilson summed up the American price of peace in this classic phrase: "We ask nothing for ourselves that we ask not for humanity." The policy of Wilson was reflected in the bold leadership of Franklin Delano Roosevelt, in the generous approach of Truman to the war-stricken of Europe and Asia, in the sagacious and cordial dealing of Eisenhower with the Allies, in the search of Secretary Dulles, East and West, for men of peace and good will. The same motive is discernible in the pre-Pearl Harbor invitation to the Japanese envoys, to meet in conference in the White House, and in Secretary Dulles' hop and skip jumps from one capital to another. It is this: that nations in conflict may meet, not as gladiators in the arena, in mortal combat; but as humans, at a round-table conference, in wisdom and understanding. This is America in the light of Europe.

27 〜

Religion in an Age of Science

I PAUSE HERE to consider with you some segments of
thought as they have come down to us in the passage of time.
The impact of the waves of thought on time leads to a consideration of religion in an age of science. My interest in the
theme, however, is not that of the historian pinpointing
facts and figures, singling out dates and events, recording
wars and victories. Nor is my objective that of the philosopher of history supplying meaning or purpose to history.
My immediate concern is a distillation of varied aspects of
human thought, made manifest in history, affecting human
life, even our lives, today.

Human thought is seed. Like seed, human thought requires time for germination, growth and development. Like
seed, human thought requires fertilization to stimulate advancement, fullness and maturity. Like seed, human thought
is conditioned by climate, mental climate; by environment,
ideas facing and surrounding an embryonic thought; by
heredity, the superstructure of tradition, the old impinging
upon the new. Usually, ideas beget ideas as generation follows generation, reproducing in the orthodox manner, according to their kind, without change or deviation. At times,
however, there is a "break" in the chain of normalcy, a de-

parture from tradition, a deviation from the standard. When that occurs, when a break has come, we call it, in the field of seeds, a freak, a sport; in the field of thought, we call it genius. Human thought has advanced more by the break of genius than by the slow steps of standard procedure.

The produce of human thought, the harvest of the mind, is garnered in written form. Call it what you please: providence, plan, or purpose; adventure, design, or accident, the best of human thought has been preserved in capsules of literary form. The ancient world is preserved and reflected in the literature of that time. Thus, the Bible is not only a great book in ethical content and moral persuasive, but a leading book in literary form and expression. All the moods of heart and mind, the wrestlings of God and man are faithfully delineated in matchless array.

The Greek world comes to life again in the legacy of Homer. The aspirations and frustrations of man, the vengeance of the Furies, the thunderbolt of Zeus are set in an imperishable form, in a literature of classic content.

Dante sums up the tradition of the Church, the life of this world and the netherworld, the vast heritage of medievalism in the outpouring of a literary form that breathes eternity.

Bible, Homer and Dante, varied in time, place, and content, have one characteristic in common. Their common denominator is man justifying God. In the broad and penetrating sweep of the ancient classics three layers of human thought are discernible:

1. An eternal quest to catch a glimpse of the unknown, unseen and unfathomable force or forces that hold this universe in balance.

2. A passionate desire to mimic, in written form, the

myriad manifestations of nature's pageantry, beauty and majesty.

3. A challenging declaration, in bold accents, of the tragedy of human existence, of the futility of man's life in a world not of his making, nor within his orbit of understanding.

Underlying them all is the one grand theme, first announced in the first chapter of Genesis: "And God saw that it was good." God justified His creation; man justifies his God.

The Renaissance is a second aspect of human thought in history. Its distinguishing characteristic is the emergence of human thought as a controlling factor in the guidance of human life. In the revelations gleaned from the ancient classics, life of man is controlled from above by fiat, by fate. Man is reconciled to his fate by faith. The Renaissance broke with that tradition and outlook.

Greek thought, the leaders of the Renaissance discovered, had evolved a form of life guided by reason. Reason for them, too, became the guiding star.

Will Durant writes, in his book *The Renaissance:*

The same century that saw the discovery of America saw the rediscovery of Greece and Rome; and the literary and philosophical transformation had far profounder results for the human spirit, than the circumnavigation and exploration of the globe. For it was the humanists, not the navigators, who liberated man from dogma, taught him to love life rather than brood about death, and made the European mind free.[1]

Life was no longer dominated from above. The benevolence of reason and the rationale of truth were accepted as the Alpha and Omega of the good and civilized life, for

---

[1]Durant, Will, *The Renaissance* (New York: Simon & Schuster, 1953), p. 86.

the men of the Renaissance. This new outlook asserted itself in creative thought in various forms and media. The discovery of the self-sufficiency of reason was like coming upon a new source of energy, unused, untapped. It was a new world in creation; created by man, in his own image, in his own design and desire.

In the wake of that discovery and creativity there was fullness of life and joy abundant; a fullness of life patterned after the Periclean age; a joy of life innocent of taboo. Reason was exalted, emotion was undervalued, and windows were opened in the direction of the acceptance of life, in the affirmation of life. Denial of life, negation of life, characteristic of the Dark and Middle Ages, came to an end with the enthusiasm that affirmed life, the stamp of the Renaissance.

This brings us to the last and concluding aspect of human thought: the modern age, or the scientific age. The modern age, recent though it is as the atomic bomb, is nonetheless linked with the Renaissance period. It had its genesis there, and is its direct descendant. Granting that the Renaissance spelled the recovery of reason; that the accent of reason was a positive affirmation of life instead of a denial, science replacing scholasticism was an inevitable logical conclusion. For once the mind was set free science became the dominating frontier of reason.

The difference in outlook between medievalism and modernism, always known to the cognoscenti, escaped the popular front until stormed by Darwin's *Origin of Species*. By that work it became evident that the difference was no longer an academic flourish, but a dividing line between the faith of the fathers and the skepticism of the sons. The faith of the fathers, grounded in the old tradition, had a world view as imaged in the Bible. It was an unquestioned fact that the Lord created the world; that He created it in six days; that man was His last and special creation. Creation by creation, fact by fact, Darwin's story is slightly different. The world, as implied in Darwin's work, is not a fixed and final creation of God; it is the effect of an evolutionary process; evolving from the simple to the complex. The duration of the world's creation, Darwin would continue, is not six days, as told in Genesis, but a duration of aeons and millennia of years. Man, finally, in the words of Darwin, was not a special last-day creation, but a freak offshoot of his brother the ape. Biology, zoology and anthropology confirmed, in their researches, the first findings of Darwin, and in their totality present a world view in conflict with the world view of Genesis.

In his recent work, *The Story of Our Civilization,* Philip Lee Ralph states:

The concept of biological evolution, documented by the relentless research of Darwin, was a revolutionary idea. . . . It arrested attention by its challenge to the traditional view of Creation. . . . Its most significant effect was to rule out the belief in a static order of nature, of a static society, or of a static universe.[2]

The end is not there. It goes beyond the apparent two world views. It asks the question announced at the beginning, a question of profound and immediate concern: What is the place of religion in an age of science? For the acceptance of the scientific world view not only retires the biblical world view, but leads to a general depreciation of religious values and concepts. If the Bible is unreliable in one place, it must be unreliable in other places, is the verdict of the

[2]Ralph, Philip Lee, *The Story of Our Civilization* (New York: E. P. Dutton, 1954), p. 236.

critic. In the face of it, it is well to ask: What is the place of religion in an age of science?

And this is the answer: The role of religion in an age of science is the same as the role of religion in any age. The apparent conflict between science and religion is largely due to the obscurity and obfuscation of the functioning of both religion and science. For, truth to tell, religion and science have more in common than in conflict. Religion and science meet in the aim underlying both: attainment of truth. They meet again in their search for the nature of reality. From Copernicus to Galileo, to Bruno, Newton and Einstein, the saga of science is the revelation of nature to man, crowned in the miracle of the splitting of the atom. They part company in their respective media, in the means they use to attain the end. The field of science is observable data, and the process is experimental, descriptive, functional. The conclusions of science are theoretical, hypothetical, relative. The field of religion is in values: human values, moral values, spiritual values. Science deals with the outer world, with the physical world, with the verifiable world. Religion deals with the inner world, with emotional experience, with data felt though not proven. Science is limited by reason, religion is an intuitive apprehension.

More significant than the theory of evolution, the evolution of the world, and of man in the world, is the moral progress of man, which the persuasives and the disciplines of religion helped to foster and develop.

The scientific age may proudly look to its achievement in the material realm; in the extension of life's comforts and luxuries on a level incomparable. All of which is and will be of increasing and lasting benefit to man, if our social structure will be sustained by the religious values of peace, justice, and love between man and man, between nation and nation.

Knock these religious values out and your façade is but a house of cards.

Otherwise stated: Religion is the foundation on which the superstructure of science is reared and built. The externalities of religion, the embroidery of religion, the rites and rituals of religion, the customs and ceremonies, which, though they vary in time and place, are perennially intertwined with religion, are but the accidents of religion, the skeleton and framework of the foundation of religion; not the essence and vitals of religion. The essence of religion is an amalgam of relationships, the sum of a threefold relationship: the relationship of man to God, the relationship of man to the universe, and the relationship of man to his brother. Man cannot escape the world in which he lives, nor the desire to be at home in the world. Man cannot escape seeking, asking: "Where is God?" Man cannot escape his brother, nor the desire to be at peace with him.

The Psalmist summed it up in one dynamic phrase: "The world is built upon the foundation of loving-kindness."

28 🐟

Freedom, or Determinism?

Two CITIES, two books, two cultures have come down to us from ancient time, and their influence has been paramount in the lives of mankind ever since. The books are the creation of two distinctive peoples: Israel and Greece.

In the mythology of Greece we meet with a son of the gods, Prometheus by name. Favored among the gods on Olympus, he was also favored among the sons of men. Favoring men, he snatched the secret of fire from heaven and brought it to man on earth. This adventure brought the wrath of Jupiter upon him. As punishment Prometheus was chained to a rock to become prey to the vultures of the sky.

Against this character of Greek mythology, it is well to juxtapose the patriarchal figure of Jacob. Jacob was not a saint. From birth to maturity he shows signs of vacillation, instability, and hesitancy, the symptoms of moral evasiveness. He cheats his brother Esau at birth; secures the birthright from him at the price of pottage; and steals a blessing from his old, blind father Isaac. He labors and struggles for the possession of his wives and children; he runs away from his father-in-law Laban; he is afraid to face his brother Esau. But the climax in the career of Jacob comes on a dark night in a wrestling match with an unknown wrestler.

The wrestling goes on all through the darkness of the night. Jacob suffers a strain in the hollow of his thigh, at the break of dawn. But when the wrestler pleads with Jacob and says: "Let me go," Jacob answers: "I will not let thee go except thou bless me." Whereupon the wrestler says to Jacob: "Thy name shall be called no more Jacob, but Israel; for thou hast striven with God and with men, and hast prevailed."

The two stories present the antithesis of Greece and Judea. Prometheus is the prototype of Greek plays and tragedies. It follows the stylized pattern of their classic writers: Euripides, Aeschylus and Sophocles. Prometheus is conceived in the theme of the classic triad: god, sin and vengeance of the Furies, that ends in tragic death. Hence, Prometheus, having sinned against Jupiter is chained to the rock, to suffer eternal death. From that fate there is no escape or retreat. Fate is irrevocable.

The character of Jacob permits the interplay of sin. Jacob falls short of sainthood. But he is not doomed because of his shortcomings. He wrestles with his fate; he wrestles all through the darkness of the night; but he surrenders not to fate; not even in the darkness of the night; not even when he is bruised and beaten in the wrestling. Jacob will not let go until he converts struggle to blessing. And the verdict of the wrestler, at the end of the match, is this: "Thou hast striven with God and with men and hast prevailed."

In the one, the deity, in whatever mythological form conceived, must have its way over man; in the other, man may wrestle with the deity and even triumph, if he is courageous enough to hold on to the ideal, to fight for a blessing. In the former, fate, predestined and preordained, seals the life of man. In the latter, the aspiration of man, the striving of man, the outreach of man, regardless of the price paid in sorrow and suffering, tips the scale in favor of man. In the one, Prometheus, having lost the favor of the gods is doomed. In the latter, man alone is the carver of his destiny. In brief, freedom of man is dramatically portrayed on two contrasting stages: The Greek myth has no concept of freedom; not even the freedom of a son of the gods on Olympus. The Hebrew legend is cast in the framework of freedom. Nothing, as symbolized by Jacob, can stop man from reaching the heights; nothing, if the ideal is battling for him. Jacob's wrestling projects the new concept: Freedom versus Determinism. Which shall it be? Judaism champions freedom of man.

Freedom to what end? Is it the freedom of anarchy, of riotous living, of life undisciplined, unrestrained, unchecked and uncurbed? Is it the freedom that knows no care, responsibility or stewardship? The anxiety of parents today, emerging from the plague of juvenile delinquency, is in no small measure due to freedom run riot, to freedom that applies no brakes, to freedom that destroys and kills. This is not the freedom that parts company with fate.

The freedom born of wrestling with fate is a positive freedom, a transfiguring and transcending freedom. It is the freedom born of self-mastery. It is the freedom born of the mastery of discipline, law and order. It is the freedom of the supreme artist: not enslaved by technique but the master of it. It is the freedom that turns its back on fate, wrestles with self, frees itself from pitfalls and road-blocks, and does not let go until the dawn of day brings blessings. It is the freedom that says: "I will not let thee go except thou bless me."

Freedom to what end?

That we may be a blessing.

29 🪶

Life's Increasing Challenge

AT TIMES LIFE is not a challenge. Where there is no self-consciousness a challenge does not exist. An animal, not being conscious of existence, experiences no challenge. For where life is guided by instinct there is no regret, and where there is no regret there is no challenge. Where life is instinctive there is no memory of the past, and no concern for the future. Where there is no future there is no challenge.

Man is self-concious. He knows that he exists, and his existence is a source of inquiry, a source of anxiety, a source of agitation. The animal does not have to justify his existence; man seeks justification. Man asks why of life, and to what end? And the more intense the inquiry the greater the goal, and the greater the goal the greater the challenge.

There is the challenge of economic security. Our needs and physical wants must be met and satisfied daily. The challenge is doubly strong when we are a man of a family; when the responsibility is not only for our own life, but the lives of wife and children, of relatives and dependents. When we know that their contentment, their peace and satisfaction depend solely on our economic gain, the challenge is inescapable.

The challenge in the economic world is not the only one.

We are social beings. Even as we crave the satisfaction of economic needs, we crave the good will of society. We crave union with our fellow man and woman. When that hunger is not satisfied, when we are not received socially, when we do not find our level among our equals, there is a ringing challenge flung at us. We ask ourselves: "Why are we isolated?"

Beyond economic needs and social satisfaction is the hunger of the mind. The mind too wants to be satisfied. For this world is an enigma, a puzzle, a riddle, a silent sphinx. Its age is a mystery, the source of its life shrouded in secrecy, its end unknown to man. The world is indifferent to man. But not so man to the world. For he has to live in the world. To live in the world is a challenge to the mind of man, who wants unceasingly to pierce the veil of the unknown.

And yet these three challenges are not to be compared with the challenge to know truth and hold fast to it. For this challenge is of spiritual fiber.

What is Truth? is an old question. Some are of the opinion that truth is relative. What may be truth in one country need not necessarily be so in another. What may be truth in one generation may not be truth in another. I grant that there is relative truth. And yet, underlying the relativity of truth there is the truth that is abiding, eternal, and universal. When a man speaks the truth it is recognized. When a woman speaks honestly, truth rests on her face. There need be no contention as to what is truth. We know what truth is when we see it. When we meet it face to face, its stamp is indelible. The real challenge is rather how to hold on to truth; how not to lose it. For truth does not always ensure economic security; in the path of truth you will not find social satisfaction; nor ease of mind.

We are told that Eve is the eternal temptress of man. Perhaps. There is, however, a temptation that escapes neither man nor woman, a temptation not of the flesh, a temptation more alluring and captivating than the most beguiling, elusive, seductive charms of woman. I have in mind the temptation of flattery, the weakness for grandeur, the hunger for power. Joseph, we are told, escaped the temptation of Potiphar, but not the temptation of being Viceroy of Egypt. No man is strong enough to see power within the grasp of his hand, and not reach for it. The visions of grandeur, the dream of power, the sweep of authority are all too alluring, too enticing, too captivating not to make a bid for them again and again, and still once again.

The attainment of that power is to be found on a forked road, for there are two ways to popular recognition and authority. The first way is to bestow favors upon the rich. When we have the means and the wherewithal it is a very easy matter to become popular. All that is necessary is to distribute wealth; to bestow it upon a chosen few. Then the dispenser of favors will be accepted among his peers; he will be well-considered. His grasp for power will come within reach of it.

The other way is to bestow charity upon the poor. When we give of our fortune to the poor and needy, there is hope that society will consider us worthy of favor and recognition.

Thus by distributing wealth to the poor and bestowing favors upon the rich we gain the opportunity to play with human souls as a child plays with his toys. And it is here, on the threshold of power and prosperity, that the ability to know truth and to hold fast to it becomes an ever increasing challenge. For the privilege of parading in the sunshine of popularity is not always on the path of truth. At times we buy social favor and recognition at the very price of honesty and truth. Popularity then becomes a cloak to conceal the very nature of our being. It is a golden apple the core of which is far from being sound. To take hold of truth in the face of temptation to power and grandeur, and to follow it, irrespective of consequences, is life's increasing challenge.

Not only in times of prosperity is it hard to hold fast to truth. In times of adversity even more so.

For society must have its idols to worship. It must have its gods to follow. The mob is willing and ready to praise Caesar — but it is no less ready to bury Caesar. It must have some one to admire, to look up to as its symbol of the adored. But the mob is equally ready to dethrone its god and burn him in effigy. To see truth and hold fast to it in the midst of wreck and ruin, in the face of adversity, that is life's increasing challenge. One must stand ready to lose favor, but not truth; to part with popularity, but not from honesty. Socrates of ancient Greece met the challenge. He saw truth and held fast to it, in popularity and adversity. He lost the favor of Athens, but not the flavor of truth. He died with the cup of hemlock in his hand rather than forsake truth.

So was Nathan in the face of David.

What does all this mean to you and to me? A great deal! For the pursuit of truth is one of the greatest aspirations of Israel. Israel could not pay a higher tribute to the pursuit of truth than to say: "The seal of the Holy One, Blessed be He, is Truth." Truth is not only the seal of God, truth is also the seal of man and woman.

It matters not what price we pay in the purchase of truth; but it does matter how we sleep at night. When we bask in the glory of popularity, when we have attained recognition, but upon our return home cannot look in the mirror of our souls, to what avail glory and popularity? Shall not our soul, in the silence of the night, be satisfied?

30 🖋

Two Festivals

WE TAKE NOTE AS the western world celebrates two festivals: Passover and Easter. The former celebrates redemption; the latter commemorates resurrection. One is the birth of a people to freedom; the other dedication to life immortal. Both festivals are celebrated in the same season of the year: in springtime, the time of the year that marks, since remote antiquity, the celebration of the summer solstice.

No record has been found of when that celebration first occurred; but whatever the time and place, it is justifiable on reasonable grounds. For it is the season of the year when the heart of man sings for joy, because nature has cast off her frozen garment and put on a robe of greenness and gladness. It is the time of the year when life springs into being. Every root in the soil is quickened by the touch of spring, every treetop is experiencing the mystery of new life. Tender flower-shoots break through earth's crust, reaching upwards to the sun; seeds, long dead in the ground, come to life, in myriad forms of growth, in varied colors and fragrance.

It is the season of the year when not only the earth is stirred; the heart of man is set fancy free; for it is springtime, and man hears the call of love. It is a season of the year best reflected in the words of King Solomon's book,

Song of Songs: "Rise up, my love, my fair one and come away! For, lo, the winter is past, the rain is over and gone; the flowers appear on the earth; the time of singing is come, and the voice of the turtle is heard in our land."

Not only the resurgence of life is manifest in the spring of the year; the freedom of life is also its token of grandeur and glory. What is life without freedom? The seed, to come to life, must break through the earth, where it is imprisoned. The bud will never come to full flower and fragrance until it is free and open. The bird cannot fly unless it breaks through the shell that imprisons it. Hence, the mystery of life, reborn in multiple forms in the spring of the year, not only evidences resurgence and renewal; it gives wings no less to the significance of life. The fullness of life is in the freedom of life.

Herein the importance of the festivals celebrated by Jew and Gentile within the span of a week. They redeem and reform, in their respective observances, the solstice celebration, the ancient festival of springtime, to modern use and understanding. Solstice and sacrifice, redemption and resurrection, point up, to modern mind, the perennial rhythm of life. Life is eternal.

In the drama of life we appear on the stage, strut and sing, act our assigned part, and then make our exit, as the curtain comes down. At times, our part in the enactment of the drama is significant; at times it is ordinary; at other times it sinks to the lowest level. To attach a transcending importance to our own particular part, to rivet attention upon our role as supremely singular and significant, is to forget that "the play is the thing."

Rising above misfortune that may hit the actors while in the play, towering above the sorrow that comes unbidden to the player on the stage is the traditional mandate: "The play must go on." Even more abiding, more continuous, and more permanent and universal is the drama of life, where the earth is the stage, and the generations of man its actors, players and performers. The actors come and go; the players mount the stage, enact their respective roles, and make their exit as they do their entrance, an unheralded cycle in the drama of life. But while some performers may come and some performers may go, the stage is never free from the generations of man. For the drama of existence is unending. Life is eternal.

In this unending drama, in the eternal web of the mystery of life, some gains have come down to us that are co-equal with life. They are co-equal with life because they are inherent in life, the very fabric of life, the conservers and preservers of life. They are moral principles, spiritual values; eternal as life is eternal. The principles are love of God and love of man; love of freedom and love of righteousness. In the pursuit and practice of these principles, life is not only enriched and ennobled, exalted and dignified, but ever anew reborn, ever more and more linked with eternity. A life rooted in the love of God and love of man, centered in the pursuit of righteousness, is a life set free from the bars of hate and ill will that imprison man and darken counsel.

Life eternal, made eternal by the plasma of moral principles that are enriching and ennobling, is the significance of the festivals that usher in the springtime of the year. To Jew and Gentile they say in the words of the sages: "For man liveth not by bread alone, but upon the utterance of the word of God." And the word of God is life eternal.

31 ✍

The Mortality of Ideas

IT IS THE TRADITION in wartime that casualty lists of those fallen by land, sea, or air are withheld from public notice until the families of the casualties have been notified. When the casualty list is finally published, we accept it submissively, resignedly, as our sacrifice to God and country.

By now we know the names and numbers of those killed in the cold war, in World War II, and in World War I. But we still do not recognize sufficiently that behind the mortality of men there is the mortality of ideas, that the death of a man in war points up the death of a moral idea, in time of peace.

The time has come to take stock, not only of the mortality of men, but of the mortality of ideas. No record has been kept of the ideas murdered, of the values slaughtered, of the principles perished. Therein the tragedy of our time, the tension of our age, the anxiety of our lives. The time has come to know that every life lost in battle is the consequence of an ideal lost in life. It is not too late yet to learn that when a man is murdered an ideal has been murdered first. Only when ideals and values are alive, in the lives of men and nations, are the lives of men safe and secure.

Consider, if you please, the mortality of ideas: The first

man killed, as recorded in the Bible, was victim of the death blow to the ideal of contentment. The first flood that wiped off all living things from the face of the earth, we are told, was the consequence of righteousness disappearing from the face of the earth. The fiery destruction of the four cities of wickedness came in the wake of a life void of justice, truth and goodness. Nature harbors no vacuum; and human life cannot long endure in a climate of suspended moral values. Either morality or immorality must prevail. Upon the exit of truth falsehood takes over; upon the death of righteousness, unrighteousness comes to life; upon the dethronement of peace, war is king.

We have escaped, thus far, in the death of values, the suspended doom; but who can guarantee that we are not next on the list? Not necessarily as draftees for the army or navy, or air corps; nor as those to be purged for no guilt or crime committed, but as victims of a social order that fails to stem the tide of corruption, of slaughter, and murder. Who knows but this strange interlude is the opening floodgate to a deluge that will engulf mankind and sweep it to utter annihilation and destruction? Who knows but our time is a prelude to a catastrophe incalculable, only because we have permitted moral development to lag behind the material and scientific?

Should we not, under the circumstances, be moved to something more than quiescence, acceptance, or watchful waiting? If the house next door were in flames, would you not be aroused? If a deadly disease attacked the family next door, would you not be concerned? And if the pillars of civilization are crumbling in Asia, how long before the pillars of Europe will crumble and collapse and affect the façade and structure of America? To appraise our convulsive time, to take cognizance of our jittery age, is to take stock of the mortality of ideas.

Evidently our military defense, our material prosperity, our scientific advancement have not lessened the mortality of war, decreased tension or the fear of tomorrow. Recognition must come that ideals and values are our safety valves. It must be made doubly clear that if totalitarianism wins, all we cherish in our spiritual heritage is lost, because in the onslaught of communism, ideals and values die first.

In the defense of the ideal is our safety and security. The Allies have missed the boat three consecutive times: We were fooled by Kaiser Wilhelm in 1914. We were cheated by Hitler in 1939. We are being pinned down in Asia by a masked truce. The time has come to recover our losses, to recapture lost ground. And our recovery has to be moral; our help is in our spiritual resources. In the recovery of spiritual values lies the recovery of peace and security. With Isaiah we conclude and say: "The effect of righteousness shall be peace, confidence and security evermore."

32

Ways of Marriage

THE CEREMONY OF MARRIAGE, to the unreflec-
tive eye, seems uniform wherever held, in church, synagogue
or cathedral. To the reflective eye, marriage takes on different forms and manifestations. It depends, now as always, as
in any other human relationship, on the character of the individual, on the nature of man.

The history of man is not of yesterday. It reaches into millennia. Nor was it yesterday that man discovered that "it is
not good for man to be alone." Ever since man became conscious of his existence, he knew that it is not good for man
to be alone. Hunger drove him in search of food; thirst im-
pelled him to dig for water; sex made him know woman.
Mating was met; hunger was satisfied.

Marriage on this plane is animalic, biological, physiological. Man, on this level, seeks his woman as he hunts his
prey. Both are to be had in any way attainable, to satisfy a
hunger. Woman on this plane is but a tool of man. She exists to satisfy his wants. Whatever worth and value woman
has is the worth and value man places upon her, as his chattel, his possession, his property. Woman as a personality
does not exist. She is the reflection of the man who owns her.

Her children are the property of the man; her body belongs to him.

Long though man remained on that level he yet advanced, in time, to a higher level. In time, it became evident that man cannot endure, society will not prosper, if woman is only the chattel of man, with no rights of her own, to shield her and protect her against the physical force of man. Thus marriage, originally little more than capture of the weak by the strong, subjugation of woman to the interest of man, assumed the form of a civil contract between man and woman, guaranteed by the prestige and authority of the state. Woman, henceforth, came to have protection before the state. She was protected by the law of the state, entitled to the defense of her civil rights by the state.

Marriage on this plane, legally contracted and legally protected, we designate civil marriage. The law projected by society becomes the invisible third partner to the contracted union of the two. By the proscription of the invisible third, the two must live; else their contract is dissolved by law as consummated by law. Civil law marriage is the highest expression of the state. It is civilized marriage. It declares woman the equal of man by law; by force, if necessary. No marriage today is entered into without the sanction of civil law. Within the frame of the law, marriage is a civil partnership between man and woman, as husband and wife, for a period of time agreeable to both. Civil marriage at its highest legalizes what biology urges.

Solemnized marriage is man's finest spiritual union. It disciplines desire and converts lust to loyalty through the alchemy of the spirit. Marriage so envisaged rises above the concept of woman made for the pleasure of man; lifts marriage above the status of a civil contract. For religion views the individual as a human personality that belongs neither to man nor to the state. Marriage as viewed by religion is more than a mating of bodies. It is a meeting of souls; and where two souls meet there is a harmony that needs no law to enforce it.

Of such a nature is marriage as viewed by Israel. Hence wedlock, in the words of Israel, is called *Kdushin* — sanctification. To Israel, marriage is a sacrament, a sanctification of life. Marital relations, it is true, may have had a very humble origin; they may be rooted in the animalic and physiological, but they need not end there. No relationship, says Israel, is too humble to be sanctified, especially human relationships, especially so private and personal a relationship as marriage. In that hope Judaism solemnizes marriage, in keeping with the custom of Moses and Israel.

And yet we know that not Judaism, but only those concerned can solemnize a marriage. For man can make marriage either a marriage of lust, a marriage of law, or a marriage of love. Which shall it be? Only the contracting parties can answer this question. The two concerned will be helped in their decision by the following considerations: A happy and lifelong marriage rests on the recognition of the equality of sexes; upon the understanding that marriage is more than mating; and upon the resolution that marriage is for life and not for the duration of a joyful experiment. The structure of civilized society, the solidarity of the family and the happiness of man are insured in marriage so conceived and so lived.

33 ❧

A Woman's Prayer

IN THE OPENING chapter of the Book of Samuel we are told that Elkanah observed at the festive meal on a festive day that his wife Hannah refused to eat, and was disconsolate, because she had no children. And although Elkanah assured Hannah that he loved her more than ten children, yet she remained uncomforted. In her sorrow she proceeded to the sanctuary at Shiloh. There she poured out her heart in prayer for a man-child.

This simple little story of a woman fasting on a festive day; this anguished heart of a wife, though truly loved by her husband; this woman's prayer for a child is as significant now as ever before. Though thousands of years have passed since this longing prayer was first uttered, though cast in a language strange and foreign to modern man, it is yet as alive, as moving and passionate as the pleadings of a man doomed to death, praying for life and liberty.

Should you ask why this woman's prayer transcends the limits of time and the barrier of language, the answer is because it is universal in its appeal and pathos. The prayer is a literary classic, though small in dimension, because it is so completely human. The story, whenever read, arrests attention, because it epitomizes the tragedy of a life unfulfilled, a

hunger unsatisfied, a life unrealized. It is the story of the
eternal hunger of the eternal woman: to become mother.

When Hannah's prayer was answered, when her hunger
was satisfied, when the barren woman became mother, she
brought her son, Samuel, in his first blush of boyhood, to the
same sanctuary where she had first prayed for a male child.
And she left her son in the care of Eli, the high priest, to
serve under him as an apprentice in the sanctuary. The
mother, apparently, was not satisfied with the mere gift of
life, with the mere possession of a son. She brought her son
to the sanctuary. Here is the inspiring difference between the
animal mother and the human mother. The animal mother
is satisfied in answering the call of nature, in reproducing
after her own kind. For mother nature has no impulse other
than recreation, reproduction, perpetuation of the species.
Nature has no moral values to preserve. Not so man; nor the
mother of man. Hannah brings her son to the sanctuary.

For a mother's prayer is answered, not in the offspring of
the flesh, but in the flesh apprenticed in the spirit of the
sanctuary. The human mother is blessed when her prayer is
answered; when the gift of life comes to her. Thrice blessed,
however, is the mother whose prayer is answered in promise
and fulfillment, when her child is not only the promised offspring of the flesh, but the fulfillment of a maturing personality that lifts human life above animal life.

A mother's prayer, so interpreted, has significance for all
mothers, of all kinds and climes. It is true that woman's
natural destiny is motherhood. But what shall be the nature
of the child who will bless her, as mother? It is true that
a mother's prayer is for new life, and more life. But what
shall be the nature of that life, and its increase? The animal
does not ask this question. Only man dares to question life.

In this very questioning is the implied answer: A mother's prayer is for more than a physical offspring. For human life is more than animalic existence. The mother of man prays for a life that will be clothed in moral values fitting the dignity of the human personality.

34 ❧

Loyalty

LOYALTY IS A GOOD and honorable word. Its meaning could be defined as "faithful in allegiance." A problem arises when we ask allegiance to what? Is the allegiance of an American citizen to Russian communism defensible, for example, on the ground of loyalty to communism?

Galsworthy's play: *Loyalties,* is profoundly concerned with this very crucial question. The author projects a British army officer, whose private life is a web of vice and corruption. But his record as an army officer is gallant and commendable. He is on trial for theft. To permit his private life to be exposed to public condemnation would reflect upon the code and character of the British Army. Loyalty to the army prompts an officer of the service to come to the rescue of the officer on trial, and to defend him, at the cost of truth, in the interest of the good of the service. Is that loyalty to the army, at the expense of honesty, defensible?

The celebrated Dreyfus case is another example of loyalty, with a suspended question mark. Captain Dreyfus of the French Army was accused by a military court in 1894 of treason and was condemned to Devil's Island. Although the evidence against Dreyfus was a tissue of falsehood, loyalty to the army labelled Dreyfus a traitor. Not until 1906 was the verdict reversed, and the dishonored captain restored to credit and dignity. Was the loyalty of the clerics to the French Army, at the expense of the honor of Dreyfus, defensible or justifiable? Perhaps the loyalty of an American citizen to communism, that of the British officer to his class, and that of the French cleric to the army, will be better understood if we pause to ask again: Loyalty to what?

Loyalty is of a multiple character, punctuated by a scale of values. Loyalty begins with the smallest cell in the circle and extends to the largest body possible. Loyalty's first response therefore, is to one's self. For self-preservation is nature's first command. Loyalty to one's self evidently precedes all other loyalties, the better to grow, mature and develop physically, mentally, and spiritually. But loyalty does not end there. Loyalty to self leads to loyalty to duty, to action, to others.

Take the duty of the man in the lighthouse, for example. It is his duty to keep the light shining for those on the high seas, for the shipwrecked and storm swept. The loyalty of the soldier on guard duty, the loyalty of the fireman to those in peril, the loyalty of the policeman — all involve the risk of life, if necessary, in the line of duty.

Rising above loyalty to duty is loyalty to our family, to our own in flesh and blood. Their care and well-being is our constant commanding interest. Loyalty to duty ends with termination of duty. Loyalty to the family never ends.

Where do these respective loyalties receive their sanction and authority? What is the source of the binding power and commanding influence that translates loyalty into duty, and duty into action? What is the fountainhead that inspires duty and refuses veto?

It is to be found in loyalty to moral values.

The first of these is truth. Loyalty to truth is stronger than loyalty to self, deeper than loyalty to civic or patriotic duty, thicker than loyalty to blood. Loyalty to truth transcends all other loyalties. It is the fountainhead of them all. Loyalty to truth is in the scientist's quest for reality in tube or telescope. It is in the artist's pursuit of his vision of a world beautiful. It is in the saint's devotion to his deity. It is a loyalty that cannot be bought or bartered. It is a loyalty that is fearless in fire or water, faithful unto death. By its standard all other loyalties are measured and appraised. It is the dynamic inspiring all loyalties.

By this criterion and process of evaluation, allegiance to communism, to a class, to a clique is nullified. Is the value of freedom, for example, served by allegiance to communism? The increasing enslavement of peoples and countries, races and religions in the orbit of communism spells the answer.

By the same token, wherever the spirit of man is crushed and the wings of liberty are clipped, loyalty to value must be the final frame of reference. Racism, bigotry, discrimination must be similarly brought before the tribunal of values. Our human values manifest themselves on a broad, positive, universal and liberating frontier.

Human values do not enslave, but emancipate man, do not segregate but integrate mankind, do not splinter, but unite the human race. Human values, in brief, ennoble life, enrich society and dignify human relationships. Loyalty to moral values, thus, is loyalty to the Highest. Man could not love God, if he would not love truth first.

Today, perhaps, as never before, man is called upon to choose between loyalty to the state — communism — and loyalty to the highest moral values. And the decision in the dilemma, the choice of man, comes in the words of Moses: "Whoever is for God," for the highest moral values of life, "let him follow God."

35 🌿

A Question That Must Be Answered

I BELIEVE IT is fair to assume that any individual with his ear to the ground will hear rumbling sounds that spell world-wide tension. It is a post-bellum tension. This global tension, broken down into spheres and areas of influence, offers a detailed view of the world we live in. There is political unrest and revolution brewing in Asia. War is waiting in Europe, resting on the threshold between East and West — Germany. There is the Korean truce, that brought neither peace nor victory. In America, we have the emergence of a Republican administration, facing a generation who have not known a Republican President.

Overshadowing global tension, an extraordinary occurrence in world affairs — an occurrence that almost stopped the hands of the clock — was the death of Stalin. The man who seemed immortal met mortality; the man who held the scales of the world in balance ended the way of all flesh; the man who held his grip on the world for the last thirty years, was himself held in the grip of *rigor mortis*. Unexpected as was the occurrence, so sharp was the instantaneous reaction to the end of Stalin's world domination that for one split second, liberty-loving people everywhere breathed a sigh of relief. Heads were raised as they learned that the sceptre of enslavement had fallen from the grasp of the enslaver. For they knew that much of the world tension was attributable to Stalin; that for thirty years, he had generated world unrest when it was in his power to bequeath world peace — had he sought peace.

When the world capitals finally recovered from the news that Stalin was no more, world strategy took a holiday, waiting to see who would be his successor. The mantle of leadership having fallen on Malenkov, men are still asking the question: Will he perpetuate Stalin's destiny, dynasty, and despotism? Perhaps it is safe to assume that for some time to come, the policy of the Kremlin and the strategy of communism will suffer no perceptible change. It is certain, however, that the slightest political match cast carelessly into the international cauldron will kindle a conflagration that could end civilization.

Beyond world tension, beyond the Kremlin's next strategy, there rises a question that must be answered. The question is not concerned with world empires, nor with world statecraft. The question is concerned with the moral nature of man. The question is: What is the moral legacy of Stalin? Do not his thirty years of enslavement, enchainment, and enfeeblement of millions of human lives, coupled with his own life of security, serenity and tranquillity, contradict the moral postulate of a God of justice and righteousness? Can you square the life of Stalin — a rule of wholesale murder, unbridled treachery, unlimited atrocity during a life which reached more than the allotted three score and ten, in perfect peace and prosperity — can you square it, I repeat, with the religious promise that morality begets prosperity, while wickedness harvests adversity? For thirty years Stalin trampled over human lives, crushed them to dust, purged all opposition to his tyrannical will, and yet he reached a rewarding ripe old age, dowered with success, sovereignty and supremacy.

Where is the God of Justice, in the life of Stalin?

Granting the claim and the protest, the valid truth remains that justice is neither refuted nor contradicted because of the treacherous life of Stalin. For the criterion, in the realm of morals, is the ideal, the principle, and not the person. Man is only a vehicle for the ideal; the ideal is not limited by man; the ideal transcends man. Man fails, but the ideal never fails; man dies, but the ideal never dies. Was freedom checked because the mighty Pharoah was the arch enslaver? Was religious freedom stopped cold, because Antiochus Epiphanes crushed all opposition to his mode of worship? Was freedom of conscience arrested, because Torquemada burned the infidels alive?

We have travelled a long road since, and so have the ideals of man. Despite temporary moral eclipse and mid-twentieth century religious relapse, moral values have been in constant, progressive ascendancy. Not only is paganism extinct, and idolatry on the way out; but freedom, despite the many road-blocks, is gaining ground; and democracy, in the face of communism, is the wave of the future. Those who would claim that the life of Stalin invalidates the ideal of justice would do well to ask themselves this simple question: "Which of the two lives would they rather emulate and follow: that of Franklin Delano Roosevelt, crippled and paralyzed President of the United States, or that of Dictator Stalin?" By their choice they affirm the permanency of moral values, the eternity of the ideal of justice.

And the Jew confirmed it, decisively and firmly, in the word of the Psalmist: "The Lord regardeth the way of the righteous; but the way of the wicked will perish."

36

Some Ideals of Love and Marriage

EVERY BOY AND GIRL who has passed through the stages of puberty and adolescence, conjures up in his or her world of fancy the image of the ideal mate each would have as a life companion. To the girl there comes the vision of her Prince Charming; the youth dreams of his Queen Celestial. Not always do these dreams come true; some do not marry the image conjured up in their early life. Has the ideal of love and marriage then escaped them? No! For ideal love is seldom, if ever, realized before marriage. If realized, it is after marriage.

Of all the human relationships possible on this earth, none is so complete, so intimate, so consummate as that of marriage. Marriage is the fullest revelation of one soul to another. Our self, our power, our achievement, our inmost and utmost potentialities lie open before the naked eye of our discerning critic, our helpmate. Not only our potentialities; our weaknesses, our defects, our limitations are no less glaringly revealed. All that we are and capable of becoming passes under the scrutiny of an eye most searching, a heart most sympathetic, a mind most helpful. In the revelation of souls, identification of interests is established, a blending of selves achieved, a harmony of lives realized. And it is upon the arrival of mutuality and identity of interest in wedded life that the ideal of love is within the realm of realization.

Within our own hands therefore lies the strange and mystic power to carve and fashion the ideal of our love through the divine alchemy of sympathy and understanding, realized in a mutuality of interest. Hence the Talmud calls the unmarried, *Plag goof,* a half person. For the unmarried is indeed only half realized. But marriage brings into bloom the finer potentialities of man and woman. True marriage makes the ideal of love realizable, possible.

We are helped in the realization of the ideal in love and marriage when marriage is not viewed as an adventure, an experiment, a trial garment to put on and to take off at will. Marriage is a union for life. Trial marriage, experimental marriage, companionate marriage is condemned *ab initio.* For the foundation of that marriage is lust, and not love. Trial marriage is rooted in the desire for temporary satisfaction conjugally. Trial marriage is a marriage of impulse and not of understanding. Trial marriage usually leads to the parting of the ways.

Marriage, to satisfy the ideal of love, must never think of divorce in reserve. That divorce is at times inevitable, at times perhaps the only solution to an insoluble marital situation, is granted. But marriage with divorce in mind is a desecration of the highest attributes of the human personality. Not only the individual; society, too, suffers from shipwrecked lives. Society cannot prosper, the home can never become the destined shrine of love, children can never receive the beneficence of devoted parents, when divorce is in ambush. Better not marry than marry with divorce in reserve. Delay marriage, if necessary, but do not risk a marriage of chance. For the ideal of love is born of marriage conceived only in terms of union and permanency.

The ideal of love in marriage is assured when marriage is a synthesis of physical attraction, plus spiritual affinity. The first command given to man is: "Increase and multiply." Nature, in its myriad manifestations of life, has no other interest except the increase of life. To that end, nature multiplies the attractions of the opposite. Once nature's end is achieved and fertility is over, her interest in the species ceases. Not so man. Man transcends nature. For man is creator of values, spiritual values. Over and above the physical attraction motivated by the earthly and elemental within him, he grafted the spiritual interest, actuated by the divinity of his soul.

Spiritual affinity is made of the intangible overtones of physical impulse, but is no less real. It is woven together of the strands of love and loyalty, kinship of interest, partnership of desires and harmony of tastes. Spiritual affinity is the aroma and fragrance of dreams, hopes and aspirations shared alike, sensed alike, suffered alike. Spiritual affinity, above all else, rests upon the rich assets of mutual respect for each other's personality. When woman is not viewed as a tool, but loved as a personality, the ideal of love in marriage is realized. Then marriage is not fleeting, but permanent. For the way to love is not, as some would have us believe, through the gastronomic channel. It is rather through the avenue of respect. Where true love abides, respect will live there too.

To the brides of yesterday, to the brides of today, and to the brides of tomorrow, I would say: For the sake of the ideal in love and marriage, live on a high spiritual plane, earn the respect of your beloved, and love will follow as day follows night. Even more will come in its wake: worship and adoration.

37 🌿

The Promised Land

THE REDWOODS of California are old, very old, ante-dating the white man's conquest and colonization of the Pacific Coast regions. The redwoods are strong and mighty. Because of their strength and size, they are the pride of the land. Yet the snail is higher in the scale of evolution than the redwood. Because the snail, though slow in motion, yet moves faster than the redwood. Locomotion is the criterion of progress. Not size, nor antiquity, but motion constitutes progress in the roll of ages.

Even so in the history of man. The history of man began when he left the trees and came down to live on earth. When our ancestors lived on the limbs of trees, leaping from branch to branch, they were like apes. When they came down the trees and began to walk, they were no longer apes, but men. Locomotion helped much to change the animal into man.

Motion is not only physical; motion is also mental. The distance between primeval man, roaming the forest with club in hand, in search of food and water, and the present social order, is the distance between the savage and the civilized. In that distance of time and space, man not only covered the earth, but conquered the earth; and much above and below it. And the history of man and nations, cultures and civilizations, is but a record of the progress of the mind from self-awareness to an awareness of the planets in the heavens above and the multiforms of life in the waters below. In the process of awareness, man has become the master of all he surveys — except one thing: Man is not yet master of himself.

He pierces the heavens in flight, he splits the sea with his craft, he corners the bolt of the sky; but he is helpless before the raging of his own heart. Master of the earth, he remains slave to his passions. Man has discovered the laws of nature, he has charted the laws of life, but the law of love is not in his heart. Hate still rules mankind, bloodshed is still the pastime of man, warfare is still the plaything of nations. Man tames the wild beast of the jungle, but he cannot live in peace with his brother.

The achievement of the mind pales in the face of destructiveness of the heart. Of what significance is the material progress of the centuries during which man advanced from savagery to civilization, if not a century was free from human conflict, national strife and international bloodshed? What pride in the twentieth century, if nearly half of it has been dedicated to death and destruction? Great is the gift of self-awareness; it marks the beginning of human consciousness. But of what avail consciousness, if it does not make us conscious of the existence of others? Great is the gift of nationalism; it has taught the love of country. But of what avail nationalism, if it has not taught us also love of other nations and peoples, countries and races? Great is the revelation of religion; it is Jacob's ladder to the heights of heaven. But of what use religion, if it has not taught us recognition, respect and reverence for the dignity of man?

Enriched with the latest discoveries of the mind, surrounded with untold wealth, deluged with endless panaceas, man today is still economically insecure, politically enslaved, religiously blind. He is still struggling for a political gospel to govern the state; still hoping for a savior to redeem society; still waiting for a miracle to lead him to the promised land.

The promised land is the heart of man. No man, no country and no race can rise higher than the promptings of the heart of man. For the heart of man is the springboard to the advancement of humanity. Of old we were told: "Above all things guard the heart; for out of the heart are the issues of life." And the need of the hour is the healing of the heart. The heart of humanity is wounded; poisoned with arrows dipped in bitterness, prejudice and ignorance. Fear covers the face of the earth, born of economic insecurity, national rivalry and racial hostility. War, cold and hot, implemented with unrivalled barbarism and savagery, is invading countries, conquering peoples, and subduing nations. Wherever you turn, hate is king; and his dominion covers the face of the earth. How are we to bring a healing balm to a bruised humanity, if not through the ministrations of the heart, through the offering of love? Hate will not save us. The promised land is the heart of man, the ministry of love.

The progress of man must be spelled in spiritual accents. Man has progressed physically. Man has moved mentally. But man reaches full stature only when he is touched by the springs of the spirit. All the stature of the body, all the wealth of the mind cannot redeem poverty of the soul. But a soul saturated with love is the savior of society. This the giants of the spirit knew full well. Hence Israel declared in accents imperishable: "Love thy neighbor as thyself." Love thy neighbor, black or white, Jew or Gentile; love thy neighbor, Christian or infidel; love thy neighbor, rich or poor.

Hillel, the sage of Israel, when asked to sum up the Law, answered: "What is hateful unto thee, unto thy neighbor, thou shalt not do" — a forerunner of the Golden Rule of a later day. Rabbi Yohanan Ben Zakai, of a still later day, when examining the attributes and virtues of man, singled out love of heart as man's supreme and transcending virtue. For, says he, in the love of the heart, all virtues of man are embraced and included. The Talmud sums up man's supreme virtue in these three words: *"Rachmanah lieba boyeh —"* God desireth the heart.

Nations, too, have hearts. The collective feelings and emotions of the citizens of a land or country become its heart. As the individuals feel so the heart of the nation responds. There can be no peace on earth if we plant ill will in the hearts of men. But peace will come to warring nations when good will inhabits the heart of man. When nationalism is rampant, racism riotous, aryanism a blessing and semitism a curse, then the heart of humanity is split asunder. But the realization that in our Father's house are many windows, all looking to the sun, opens the road to the promised land, heralds peace to mankind, and fills the heart of man with love of God and love of man. That the dawn of that day may not be too distant is the prayer of Israel, the hope of humanity.

38

The Crumbling Pillars

IT IS WELL that we meet to give thanks to our Father in Heaven. No man can live by himself; no people can cut itself off from the current of the times; no country can isolate itself from the world atmosphere about it. Even Chinese walls are no longer safe and secure. That we are permitted, as free men in America, to pause and reflect upon world conditions is in itself a source of praise and thanksgiving. Not in totalitarian Europe will you find such freedom. In America we dare face the world and society and declare: The pillars of the world are crumbling!

What are these crumbling pillars?

The word *progress* is synonymous with the unfolding and flowering of the human race. From quadruped to biped; from cave dwelling to crowded cities; from animal hunting to interlocking trusts; from crude hand scratching to inventive genius; from savagery to sainthood advance the steps of progress. The gigantic strides taken in the avenues of human adventure: scientific, spiritual and cultural, are reflected and embraced in the word progress. Beginning, however, with the Industrial Revolution, the word progress gradually loses its ideal content and becomes more and more freighted with material advancement and achievement. Progress, from then on, spells a change from handwork to factory production; from steam to electricity, from man to mechanism. The consequence of that change was the emergence of the laissez-faire principle, the ideal of rugged individualism, the concentration of much wealth in the hands of a few.

During those many decades of material progress, man's economic scale of life rose considerably, but a cleavage inevitably set in. Society was divided and stratified by a new invisible power: great wealth controlling great masses of people. The masses, because of their dependence on wealth, on employment, on labor, gradually lost their status as human beings, as individuals, as personalities. They became tools in the great enterprise of commercial supremacy, cogs in the wheels of industry, commodities in the labor market, to be dealt with as the law of supply and demand dictates. Thus came the birth of class consciousness; the clash of labor with capital; the emergence of capitalism and socialism; the birth of communism.

Democracy, perhaps the finest socio-political concept of modern times, is the second crumbling pillar we now face. Democracy, defined politically as government by the consent of the governed; defined socially as civil equality before the law, though in its contemporary form and use only a hundred and fifty years old, has a record co-equal with the first promptings and aspirations of the human race. The Hebrew genius was sensitive to it with the declaration: "One law, one statute for the citizen and sojourner." Jesus expressed it nobly when he said: "Inasmuch as ye have done it unto the least of these, my brethren, ye have done it unto me".... Plato visioned it in his *Republic,* and Aristotle dealt with it in his essay on *Politics.* We catch a first glimpse of it in Europe in the Magna Carta of England; it rises in resplendent form on the western hemisphere in the American Revolution; it celebrates its rebirth and resurgence in the Revolution of France. Today, the country where democracy first had its home in Europe, France, is in a state of tension. In England, the mother of Parliaments, democracy is pitted against socialism. In America democracy is on trial.

The factor that preconditioned the collapse of democracy in Europe was not the blitzkrieg of Hitler, but the dynamic and explosive of the Forgotten Man. At every great social upheaval, whenever the pillars of the social structure crumbled, it was the restlessness, the economic insecurity, the suffering of the masses that conditioned it. So it was in turbulent England in the early decades of the thirteenth century. So it fared in revolutionary France, when the masses had no bread, but royalty had cake. So it was in precommunistic Russia, when entrenched privilege feasted on exploited peasants.

Turbulent times are society's lot when it fails to balance political democracy with economic democracy. Said Henry A. Wallace, when vice-president of the United States: "Though we in the United States have attained a fair measure of political democracy, we have done very little in perfecting a genuine economic democracy." The novel, *Grapes of Wrath,* tells the sad and disturbing plight of the sharecroppers in America, as the ever-present unemployed millions tell a story of hunger for bread that political democratic equality cannot satisfy. When a man asks: "What is the use of democracy, if I have no job? I cannot eat democracy. I want bread, for my wife and for my little ones," the seeds of communism are taking root.

One more crumbling pillar we face: the pillar of religion. Always, in the hour of distress, the fool said, in the words of the Psalmist: "There is no God." Did not the wife of Job tempt him in the hour of his great sorrow, with the words:

"Curse God and die"? The severest breakdown of faith comes when a great segment of the human family experiences a shocking disturbance. It happened in France, in the midst of the clash and crash of the Revolution. It was then that the God of mankind, the God of the universe, was dethroned, and the goddess of reason enthroned. It happened again in Russia, when the dynasty of the Romanovs gave way to the leadership of Lenin and Trotsky. There, not even a substitute for God was sought or invoked. In Russia, religion is not only doomed but taboo; an act of treason punishable by the state. In East Germany religion faces total eclipse. And wherever communism is gaining a foothold there religion is at the end of the road.

How will we save these crumbling pillars of progress, democracy and religion? By a detour from interest in the self to interest in others; by new accent given to the term *Man*.

Samson, blind and engrossed in his personal fate, caused the pillars of the Temple to crumble and thousands of people to perish. Always, those short of vision, blinded by their own personal interests, whether they seek "peace in our own time," *"Lebensraum,"* or an ocean for their back yard, are undermining the pillars of the Temple. "Where there is no vision, a people must perish." But transfigured by a vision of the grandeur and glory of man: man, a composite of things earthly and heavenly; man, a blending of finite matter with spirit infinite; man, mortal yet immortal, the Temple of Society is firm and secure.

Always mankind leaped forward when the glory of man was at the forefront. So it was when amidst spiritual chaos and darkness the genius of Israel declared: "Man is made in the image of God." So it was centuries later, when in a world of paganism Christianity declared: Jesus, though man, is God incarnate. So it was again later, when in the age of cultural darkness, the Renaissance kindled the torch of light by recovering the lost glory of the spirit of man.

A decisive contest is facing mankind today; a new world is being born. Either totalitarianism or democracy will emerge from this human travail. We know the nature of the one; the pattern is clear cut and terrifying. It spells the end of human dignity; the enslavement of mankind. The other opens the door to human freedom; it insures the enhancement of the human personality. We will fortify the strongholds of progress, democracy and religion, not by political panaceas, party platforms, or economic palliatives, but by proper and fitting appraisal of the nature of man; the only deciding and contrasting difference between the totalitarian way and the American way. The one views man as a tool, a mechanism, the property of the state. The other evaluates man as a free agent, an evolving personality, a spark divine. And only that form of government which clothes man with the prerogatives and privileges befitting the human personality, and guarantees their satisfaction, will live and prosper long after the others have failed and perished.

You ask: What can I do about it? You ask: What is the meaning of this shower of words, in terms of practical application? And the answer is: "As a man thinketh, so it is." Today we give thanks to God, above all else, for the indisputable fact that the world crisis mankind now faces is not God-made, but man-made. We willed it into being. We willed it into being when we measured progress by the size and strength of purse and power, rather than by the depth and breadth of the spirit. We willed it into being when we made democracy a political shibboleth rather than a living reality. We willed it into being when we made religion an organization, rather than a sacrament, a communion with

God and man. And we give thanks today for one more indisputable fact: What by man is made, by man can be unmade. Hence, "As a man thinketh, so it will be." In our hands lies the fate of America, the fate of mankind. Only a people that believes in human progress can and will defend human progress. Only a people that believes in democracy as all-embracing, economic no less than political, can and will defend democracy. Only a people that believes in religion, a recognition of the oneness of God and the oneness of mankind, can and will defend religion. According to our faith in and practice of these American ideals, so will it be. And for the power and privilege so to shape our course and destiny, that the torch of Liberty in America may become the torch of the world, the torch of humanity, we offer praise and thanksgiving to God — Our Heavenly Father.

39 🙈

A Blueprint for Tomorrow

THE INCREASING YEARS of America's independence have given much reason for annual rejoicing on the Fourth of July. Today America is, perhaps, privileged to celebrate the Fourth on a scale never rivalled before. Once a trembling and fearful group of Colonial rebels on a narrow strip of land on the Atlantic shore, America has become, in our day, the most formidable nation on earth. America's territorial boundaries extend to Berlin in Europe, to Tokyo in Asia; her political power covers the face of the earth; her wealth makes the other nations beggars at the door. Withdraw American influence from the world capitals, and decay, paralysis and stagnation will follow.

But even in the animal world the much coveted combination of growth, size and power alone does not constitute greatness. The record points to the contrary. The extinction of the mammoth, the dinosaur, the mastodon, for example, was accounted for by the naturalists as due to overgrowth in weight and size. The decline of nations and the death of civilizations, Gibbons, Spengler and Toynbee imply, was occasioned by power grown rampant, by size bursting at the seams. Before our own eyes Germany became an empty shell and Japan a husk of an empire after a period of surpassing military strength, exceeding territorial growth and over-reaching political power. No! Material size, strength and power, though highly desirable in man and in nation, do not in themselves constitute greatness; at times, when full blown, they carry the seeds of their own destruction. If, therefore, as Americans we celebrate America's achievements of yesterday, let us also make a worthy blueprint for tomorrow.

It is not too late to recall that the American Declaration of Independence, when first proclaimed, was not in consequence of a desire for size, growth or power. The dynamic underlying that declaration was a passion for freedom. The Declaration of Independence blazed a new frontier, the sovereignty of a people. In this concept of sovereignty, man and state were integrated; political and civil rights were fused as one; political and economic equality merged and balanced. It was not in the mind of the Founding Fathers that freedom was divisible; that the sovereignty of a state could be had at the denial of the sovereignty of man; that political equality could exist side by side with a denial of equality of opportunity. They were neither naive nor sophomoric in their declaration that: "All men are created free and equal."

At that historic occasion they rose above the dialectic that speaks with finality of environmental factors, hereditary conditions, economic circumstances. They thought of man, universal man, and declared him, as of right, and in his own right, free and equal. They were not visionaries, dreamers or crackpots when they proclaimed that life, liberty and the pursuit of happiness are man's unalienable rights. They were the champions of the rights of man; to be secured, not as a donation, but as his birthright, not to be denied by any state or power. The pattern of liberty was one for man and for state. In the mosaic of freedom there was no dichotomy between the prerogatives of the state and the privileges of man. Freedom of man and freedom of state were all wrapped in one neat package: the Declaration of Independence. It was inevitable, under the dynamic conception of freedom, that the Bill of Rights should blossom beside the Declaration of Independence. Together they spell the truth that the sovereignty of the state and the rights of man are one.

Experience confirms the interdependence of these rights: man and the state. Only where these rights interlace and act as check and balance, one against the other, are the safety of the state and the integrity of man sustained and preserved. But where man, as an individual, is not free, not independent in his own rights as man, regardless how strong the state is militarily and economically, the state is not a free state. For the criterion of a free state is the independence of man. Man is not only the measure of all things; he is the dynamic of all things; his independence not the least among them. In that understanding the Declaration of Independence remains America's bluprint for tomorrow, safeguarding the future as it insured and protected the past, with liberty and justice for all.

40

The One and the Many

THE INTERDEPENDENCE of man and state, imbedded in the Declaration of Independence, is responsible for the evolution of the political pattern of the one and the many, in the life of America. This pattern accounts for the cultural differences and racial distinctions in the mosaic of America. In the city of Washington, where the representatives of all nations have their homes, there is held a periodic pageant, called: "All Nations Festival." The variety of its program accentuates the distinctive cultural contributions to America of many nations, in costume, dance and music.

The American Indians, for example, decorate themselves with paint and feathers and emerge from their pitched tents to perform the ritual of the rain-dance, to sombre time-beating on tom-toms. The Greeks appear in their white skirts and gaily decorated tunics, with black fezzes snugly perched on the top of their heads, and dance male to male, arm to arm in squares and circles, to music, first sounded, perhaps, by the ancient Athenians. The American Negroes delight in their zoot suits, swinging arms and shuffling legs, as if they were not their own, breaking out in a dance spirited and sensuous, bursting forth in song that is as spiritual as satanic. These and many others in the exhibit are proud to display their native costumes and dances. But even though they proudly cherish their national origins, and are happy to appear in the respective art forms characteristic of their native cultures, they are happiest when they are called American; when they are identified with the cultural forms of their native or adopted country: America.

This pride in the culture of their native land; this love of the country of their adoption is not an exhibit of opposites, a demonstration of contradictions. It is the story of America. America, it is well to remember, was first peopled by men and women not native to this land. In the words of Franklin Delano Roosevelt: "As Americans, we are all immigrants, or the children of immigrants." The difference between those who arrived on the Mayflower and those who came in steerage is, as often stated before, only a difference in the time schedule. And ever since the Pilgrims first hugged the rock of Plymouth, every immigrant to these shores brought with him not only his body, but his beliefs; not only his strength, but his spirit; not only the labor of his hands, but also the hope of his heart.

These inward treasures of heart and mind, in whatever form or ritual carried across to these shores, have never been suppressed by conformity to a native culture. Alongside the native indigenous growth, other plants were permitted to blossom, and the result is a panorama of growth rich in color, surpassing in beauty, delightful in harmony. In the variety of the differences is the grandeur of the American mosaic. In the blend of multiple cultures, encouraged and sustained, the American pattern of unity amidst diversity finds anchorage. The instrument of oneness emerges out of the right for differences.

This is the significance, perhaps, of the motto on the seal

of America: *e pluribus unum*. The constitutional fathers of America not only sought to bring the many colonies into one commonwealth; they also hoped to integrate the hopes and aspirations, the heterogeneous cultural patterns and varied religious affirmations of the colonies into a national pattern that would achieve homogeneity, yet not at the price of conformity. They valued independence as they abhorred regimentation; the freedom of the state and the independence of man was their objective.

To achieve the one and to guard against the other they hitched their chariot to a star not yet born; to a cluster of thirteen nebulae. Out of many blinking starlets they looked for the crystallization of one luminous star: The United States. How well they achieved let the record of our years of independence speak. Let it speak of the growth of the states numerically, of the expansion of the national domain territorially. Let it speak of the increased population, industrial development, scientific advancement. Let it speak of the food it harvests, the wealth it has gathered, the strength of its power. Let it speak of its struggle against enslavement, its battle for freedom, its victory in war. Above all, let it speak of the determination to remain true to the resolution of the Founding Fathers declaring for the freedom of the state, for the independence of man, and for the integration of the one in the many.

41🦕

Religion in an Age of Crisis

A FUTURE HISTORIAN, examining our trying, troubling time, will be tempted to characterize it as the age of atomic production, embellished with religious trimmings. He will arrive at his conclusion through study of the data observable in our time. No need to marshal the facts of atomic production; they are known to every school boy. But it is interesting to observe religion challenging attention on many fronts. Colleges and universities are devoting time to religious emphasis; industry is engaging chaplains as members of the managerial staff (to help solve the knotty problems of capital and labor in a climate exposed to religious mediation); a revised translation of the Bible sold millions of copies in a few days, and the demand is still greater than the supply. We are, apparently, witness to a religious renaissance in an age fraught with the menace of an international crisis.

Apparently, but not factually: External symptoms are not always revelatory of internal conditions; hardly ever in the realm of religion. Beyond the outward manifestation there is great need for inner conviction. There is vital need for the conviction that religion is not the invention of priestcraft, the child of superstition, the forfeiture of reason. More than ever before, this age of crisis needs the recognition and understanding that religion is an organic part of human nature, basic to civilized society, a catalytic agent in social relations. Otherwise stated, the rationalism of the eighteenth century that gave birth to the notion that religion lost its reason, has faded out. Moreover, the fading out came about not through the strategy of the sponsors of religion, nor by the connivance of the emissaries of theology; but by the reasoning process and rational dimension of scientific advancement. Gone is the conflict between science and religion. Leading scientists of today are in harmony with the leading liberal concepts of religion.

There is but one area where religion is disgraced; but one spot where religion is dishonored; but one world where religion is discredited. It is the world of communism. How else could the Kremlin enslave the masses, cut off channels of freedom, stifle religious aspiration, if not by declaring that "religion is the opiate of the masses"? Lenin knew that the enslavement of the masses is in the choice between the life of religion or the death of religion. For no man, or masses of men, can serve both God and the state. Lenin decreed for the death of religion, to cut off rivalry for the mastery of the masses. Since then, religion is taboo in Russia. In the Kremlin, the commissar is god and king.

The fate of the masses of Russia will be the fate of the masses everywhere, if the masquerading of religion and not the idealism of religious conviction is the dynamic of our life. Democracy, political idealism fronting for religious idealism, rests on the religious conviction of the dignity of man; a religious value banished from communism. And where that religious value ends, enslavement of man begins. Where man has been robbed of his innate rights and privileges, where man has been denied the dignity of human personality, and shorn of his sonship with God, the religious conviction that it is in the power of man to rise and answer the call of destiny is crushed. But where democracy holds sway, where man is free, and the heart and mind of man are given wings to fly, there, religious conviction plays its role in inspiring man to ever greater hopes and nobler achievements in the advancement of human life.

A world in crisis may have abolished the model T in motor transportation, leeches in medicine, and log cabins as model homes; but not the excellence of religious conviction, nor the efficacy of moral values. Truth is ever more necessary; and we need the enthusiasm of religious conviction for the supremacy of Truth to prevail in human relations. There is no substitute for love; and we need the exultation of conviction that love enriches, ennobles, and enhances human life. Justice and righteousness are still the twin pillars of our social structure; and we need the weight of conviction to insure the solidity of that foundation, and the stability of human progress.

Facing the crisis of our time, we say with Elijah, facing the crisis of his day: "How long will you leap over two thresholds?" If democracy is our political stamp, let us live by the religious conviction that inspires democracy, and not by the religious trimmings of our day, that would pass as religion. If the masses of men are to be free, equality of man insured, and human dignity enshrined, the persuasives and disciplines of religious conviction will have to claim our lives, as free men in a free world.

42 ❦

The Unfinished Task

I INVITE YOUR ATTENTION to some singular occurences in the last eight years. World War II was over in 1945; but world peace was still to come. Toward that end, the United Nations was founded shortly afterward. Before the victors were able to achieve peace with the vanquished, conflict among the victors themselves appeared on the horizon, climaxing in the Korean War. A truce, finally reached, robbed the United Nations forces of their hard-earned military advantage; gained for the enemy time for regrouping on another front; and brought to America neither peace nor victory. The United Nations, far from being the arbiter of nations and the citadel of world peace, has become the sounding board of favorite ideologies, increasingly conflicting and confusing. America, though fronting a new administration, faces the same old dilemma, seeking an answer to the same old question: Should we wage war, sue for peace, or be satisfied with containment?

This unfinished task facing America, the United Nations, and peace-loving peoples everywhere involves more than a military indecision. To America, in particular, the indecision is revelatory of a suspicious split in the body-politic of the country. America is menaced externally by a formidable power; it is threatened internally by subversive influences. Compounded, it is a situation that imparts a sense of inadequacy abroad, a touch of insecurity at home. A foreign nation, determined upon world conquest, is on the march, and there are no road-blocks to stop it. Since 1945 a dozen nations, involving eight hundred million people, have been swept up by this road march, without a single declaration of war. The total cost of that march is not in sight yet. For the first time in the history of man, the western world stands in fear of the shadow of the eastern world.

The fear is not in the loss of people or territory, but in the onsweep of an ideology devastating to our cherished hopes and aspirations. We are witness to the tragedy that spells out the utter corruption of man's noblest ideals, and the ascendency of a totalitarian doctrine that declares war peace, slavery freedom, and falsehood truth. We are face to face with a world in the making where terror, treachery, and tyranny are the ruling power. We are neighbor to a police state that cripples, paralyzes and handcuffs the strongest arms.

How did it happen? you ask. And this is the answer: It was achieved by crushing the conscience of man. Silence the moral sense and all else is possible. The softening process initiated by Hitler, a score of years ago, is still going strong. Ever since England refused in 1939, on the plea of France, to stop Hitler's legions from crossing the demilitarized area between Germany and France, concession and appeasement became the goosestep of nations. The net return of the declining decades from Munich to Yalta to Vietnam is a progressive weakening of the conscience of man, leading to a blackout of the moral law, a fade-out of the conscience from the heart of nations.

The vacuum created by the exit of the moral order has

been filled by the invasion of a military order that feeds upon violence and destruction, confirming the age-old truth, that history is one everlasting repeat performance. For the history of man teaches one constant lesson: If man refuses to follow the moral order and be free, he will inevitably follow the immoral order and be enslaved. Facing the dilemma of our decade, the choice between freedom and enslavement, the unfinished task is crystal clear: dedication to the freedom of man. The dynamic underlying freedom, however, is the moral mandate — that proclaims the dignity of man. The passion for freedom must be fired by the passion for human dignity. The pleadings of former President Hoover are most timely and persuasive. "Our freedom," says he, "can be saved only by a spiritual mobilization." To which, may I be permitted to add: only a spiritual mobilization will sweep clean the subversive termites from our land within, and energize our forces to challenge the unleashed tyranny abroad.

We must marshal our forces for the triumph of the moral spirit. Basic to preparedness, to defense, to armament is spiritual armament. Fortified with moral integrity we are unconquerable. The ideals and values that imparted brilliance to the age of the Renaissance, vigor to the period of the Enlightenment, courage to the American Revolution, and fortitude to the French Revolution, must once again become the aspiration and inspiration of our time and day; the aspiration of free men in a free world. I am confirmed in this hope by the words of the prophet: "Ye shall prevail, not by might, nor by force, but by my spirit, says the Lord."